MW01131588

MY CONFESSION HANDBOOK, JR.

A Child's Worry-Free Handbook to the Treasure
of the Sacrament of Reconciliation
Great for Saints-In-Training, Ages 7 – 10,
With the Guidance of Parent or Guardian

KRISTEN M. SOLEY

...In all things, love - St. Augustine of Hippo

WESTBOW°
PRESS
A DIVISION OF THOMAS NELSON
& ZONDERVAN

Copyright © 2015 Kristen Marie Soley.

All rights reserved. No part of this book may be used or reproduced by any means, graphic, electronic, or mechanical, including photocopying, recording, taping or by any information storage retrieval system without the written permission of the publisher except in the case of brief quotations embodied in critical articles and reviews.

Diary of St. Maria Faustina Kowalska: Divine Mercy in My Soul © 1987 Marian Fathers of the Immaculate Conception of the B.V.M. All Rights Reserved. Used with permission.

WestBow Press books may be ordered through booksellers or by contacting:

WestBow Press
A Division of Thomas Nelson & Zondervan
1663 Liberty Drive
Bloomington, IN 47403
www.westbowpress.com
1 (866) 928-1240

Because of the dynamic nature of the Internet, any web addresses or links contained in this book may have changed since publication and may no longer be valid. The views expressed in this work are solely those of the author and do not necessarily reflect the views of the publisher, and the publisher hereby disclaims any responsibility for them.

Any people depicted in stock imagery provided by Thinkstock are models, and such images are being used for illustrative purposes only. Certain stock imagery © Thinkstock.

ISBN: 978-1-4908-7664-1 (sc)
ISBN: 978-1-4908-7665-8 (hc)
ISBN: 978-1-4908-7663-4 (e)

Library of Congress Control Number: 2015906009

Print information available on the last page.

WestBow Press rev. date: 06/09/2015

Author family photo by Tina Fisher Photography

ARCHDIOCESE
OF
SAINT PAUL &
MINNEAPOLIS

Title: My Confession Handbook, Jr.

Author: Kristen M. Soley

Publisher: Westbow Press

Pages: 100

Category: Catechetical – devotional

Comments: Requested changes having been made, a *nihil obstat* is now in order.

NIHIL OBSTAT _____
            Rev. George Welzbacher
            Censor librorum

DATE: 2/5/15

IMPRIMATUR _____
            The Most Reverend John C. Nienstedt
            Archbishop of St. Paul and Minneapolis

DATE: 2/5/15

226 Summit Avenue | Saint Paul, MN 55102-2197 | T: 651.291.4400 | F: 651.290.1629 | www.archspm.org

Contents

In Thanks

This handbook was made possible through the inspiration of the Good God, the Divine Healer and Friend of Sinners, and the prayers of Our Blessed Mother.

Thank you God for my husband & best friend Nate, for encouraging me to write, and for our seven beautiful children.

I am grateful for my spiritual directors and confessors: Fr. Joseph Johnson, Fr. David Hennen, Fr. Kenneth O'Hotto, Fr. Timothy Cloutier, Lori Knuth, and Susanne Kenton, for through their constant 'Yes' to God, I have grown closer to Him.

I am grateful for Fran Bogema (my Mom), Annie Ballalatak, Susan Mielke, Tina Fisher, my 'holy mom' friends, and Mary Hagar. God spoils me through the people He has placed on my path.

Thank you for my sisters, Monica Skoogman, Michelle Gulsvig, and Annie Ballalatak; your willingness to donate bone marrow for my bone marrow transplant - my second birthday!

Thank you Fr. George Welzbacher, for your patience and time on this project.

Ad Majorem Dei Gloriam - AMDG - *For the Greater Glory of God*

Introduction

For Parent and Child

The goal of *My Confession Handbook, Jr.* is to help our children, godchildren, grandchildren, nieces, nephews, brothers, sisters, and friends receive the Sacrament of Reconciliation with peace and joy. It is intended to reduce the fear that sometimes accompanies this sacrament, especially the first time.

My Confession Handbook, Jr. hopes to accomplish this with the following components:

- a personal commitment to receive the Sacrament of Reconciliation regularly
- a straight-forward examination of conscience
- "My Confession Worksheet," an easy, step-by-step, how-to while in the confessional, including an Act of Contrition
- a family-centered, Daily Examen to help grow in virtue and prepare for regular reception of the Sacrament of Reconciliation
- a Child's Prayer of Surrender
- a quick and easy go-to of treasured, traditional Catholic prayers

As a family, we value the Sacrament of Reconciliation and fully embrace the Church's teaching on this powerful and freeing sacrament. For many, it is an undiscovered gem in the vast treasure chest of our Church. If we can foster a love for this Sacrament in our children when they are young, they will be stronger in their faith and have a well-formed conscience when they enter the world as an adult.

As my spiritual director correctly put it, "As parents, our God-given role is the highest calling! We are called to shape character, instill virtues, and affect the world."[1] If our children are going to be well-formed, virtuous, and obedient to God in their adult years, we will have to guide their souls into a loving relationship with Jesus in their formative years.

Jesus *is* love, and He is the King of Mercy. In their humanity, our children's human weakness, they will need the assurance that they are loved and forgiven, because they most assuredly will fall, again, and again. Each time they fall, Jesus will be there in the Sacrament of Reconciliation, waiting with love and mercy, to pick them up and help them to begin again. Our children will grow, with confidence in Jesus' mercy and love through this amazing treasure!

As Catholics and children of God, we can approach this powerful sacrament with faith in the words that Jesus shared with St. Faustina.

> Daughter, when you go to confession, to this fountain of My mercy, the Blood and Water which came forth from My Heart always flow down upon your soul and ennoble it. Every time you go to confession, immerse yourself entirely in My mercy, with great trust, so that I may pour the bounty of My grace into your soul.

---

[1] Lori Knuth

"The confession of evil works is the first beginning of good works."—St. Augustine

When you approach the confessional, know this, that I myself am waiting there for you. I am only hidden by the priest, but I myself act in your soul. Here the misery of the soul meets the God of mercy. Tell souls that from this fount of mercy souls draw graces solely with the vessel of trust. If their trust is great, there is no limit to My generosity.[2]

Go, with confidence, and meet Jesus in the Sacrament of Reconciliation.

How to Use *My Confession Handbook, Jr.*

Before receiving the Sacrament of Reconciliation, sit with your child and walk through the "Examination of Conscience." (Chapter 2) Remember that your child is not required to share his or her sins with you. Next, walk your child through each step in receiving the sacrament. (Chapter 3) Providing guidance in filling out "My Confession Worksheet" (Chapter 4) will bolster your child's confidence and prepare him or her to receive the sacrament. Do not ask to see what your child has written on his or her worksheet. Tell your child that what he or she has written is something that is between God and the child. It is secret. If possible, do this for the first year, or until your child is ready to do this on his or her own.

Using *My Confession Handbook, Jr.* should enable your child to enjoy several years of worry-free confession, until he or she is ready for *My Confession Handbook,* the second book in this series created for saints-in-training, ages ten and older.

---

[2] Divine Mercy in My Soul, Diary of Saint Maria Fausinta Kowalska, Faustina Kowalska

"The confession of evil works is the first beginning of good works."—St. Augustine

CHAPTER 1

My Commitment

Sit down with your parent or guardian and make a commitment to receive the Sacrament of Reconciliation at least one time per month (e.g., the first Saturday of each month) and set this as part of your own personal commitment. Check your local church bulletin for times the sacrament is offered, and determine which is best for your family. If possible, encourage your entire family to go.

You can also go to www.myconfessioncompanion.com to download a printable Commitment Card you can frame or hang in your home.

Commitment Card

I, _____ will help _____ receive the

      (parent or guardian)   *(child's name)*

Sacrament of Reconciliation _____ time(s)

                   (# of times)

per month, on the _____

                   (first, second, third, and/or fourth)

_____ of each month.

      (day of week)

_____   _____

Parent's / Guardian's Signature(s)   Date

_____   _____

Child Signature   Date

"The confession of evil works is the first beginning of good works."—St. Augustine

CHAPTER 2

Examination of Conscience

 To make a good confession, sit down and review what you have been doing since the last time you received the Sacrament. Making an examination of conscience will help you determine in what ways you have offended God through choosing your will over His, something also known as sin.

Step 1

Pray a simple prayer, such as "Come, Holy Spirit. Please open my heart and mind to all of the ways I have offended You and hurt our Church through sin since my last confession."

Step 2

Use questions (below) to help make a good Examination of Conscience.

Use "My Confession Worksheet" (Chapter 4) to answer the following questions. Use the check mark to easily identify sins committed, and write the number of times you committed each sin. If you don't remember *exactly* how many times, you can use the terms, *few* or *many*.

You can also write any questions you have for the priest in "My Confession Worksheet."

The Lord says, "You shall love the Lord Your God with your whole heart."[3]
Did I obey God right away?
Did I doubt God's love for me?
Did I use all the graces God gave me to become closer to Him?
Did I pray my daily prayers (morning, evening, meals)?
Did I put other things before God (friends, toys, games, and money)?
Did I spend money unwisely?
Did I try to do my best for Jesus, even when I had to do things I didn't want to?
Did I place my faith in God only (not in good luck charms, etc.)?
Did I say God's name in anger or frustration or speak disrespectfully of God or Our Lady?
Did I use any bad words (swear words)?
Did I show reverence toward sacred persons, places, and things (e.g., the Pope, Bishop, priests, nuns, brothers, crucifixes, sacramentals)?
Did I miss Mass on purpose on a Sunday or Holy Day of Obligation?
Was I late for Mass on Sunday or did my behavior play a factor in our being late for Mass?
Have I abstained and fasted according to Church teaching (one hour before receiving Jesus in Eucharist, no meat on Friday during Lent, etc.)?
Did I laugh or distract others in church?
The Lord Says, "You shall love your neighbor as yourself."
Did I give my parent, guardian, or teacher right-away obedience?
Was I disrespectful to my parent, guardian, or teacher?
Did I do my chores without grumbling or needing to be nagged?
Did I speak uncharitably to anybody (parent, guardian, teacher, friend, sibling, etc.)?
Did I lie?

---

[3] God's covenant with Moses, Church of St. Paul – Examination of Conscience & Apostolate for Family consecration - Examination of Conscience

"The confession of evil works is the first beginning of good works."—St. Augustine

Did I take something that did not belong to me?
Did I tease anybody?
Did I hurt anybody?
Did I not treat my body, a temple of the Holy Spirit, with respect (eat too much, dress immodestly, avoid exercise, etc.)?
Did I respect others' personal space?
Did I say unkind words to or about someone else?
Was I envious of something someone else has or has achieved?
Did I become angry or envious and not handle my feelings in a positive way?
Was I prideful or boastful?
Could I have helped someone and chose not to?
Could I have shared and chose not to?
Could I have been charitable and chose not to?

(Note to parent or guardian, for the first several times your child receives the sacrament, walk him or her through "My Confession Worksheet" to be sure he or she understands the questions.)

Step 3 Thank God for the grace to make a good Examination of Conscience. A simple, "Thank you, God" or praying "The Glory Be" (Chapter 7) is sufficient.

Step 4 Pray to the Holy Spirit for wisdom for your confessor, that he may guide your soul closer to Jesus through the Sacrament of Reconciliation.

"The confession of evil works is the first beginning of good works."—*St. Augustine*

CHAPTER 3

The Sacrament of Reconciliation

You have completed your Examination of Conscience and are now ready to receive the Sacrament of Reconciliation!

Step 1   Meet the priest where he waits to hear your confession. You may kneel at the screen or sit to talk face-to-face with the priest.

Step 2   The priest will greet you. Begin your Confession with the Sign of the Cross and say, "In the name of the Father, and of the Son, and of the Holy Spirit. Bless me, Father, for I have sinned this is my first Confession." Or "Bless me, Father, for I have sinned, my last Confession was _____ (weeks, months, years) ago."

Step 3   The priest may read a passage from Holy Scripture.

Step 4   Use "My Confession Worksheet" to confess your sins. After confessing your sins, you may conclude by saying, "I am sorry for these and all of my sins."

Step 5   If you have prepared any questions for the priest, now is the time to ask him.

Step 6   Listen to the words of the priest. He will assign you a penance.

Step 7

Next you will be asked to pray an Act of Contrition.

An Act of Contrition

O my God, I am sorry for my sins with all my heart. In choosing to do wrong and failing to do good, I have sinned against You whom I should love above all things. I firmly intend, with Your help to do penance, to sin no more, and to avoid whatever leads me to sin. Our Savior Jesus Christ suffered and died for us. In His Name, my God, have mercy. Amen.

Or

O my God, I am heartily sorry for having offended You and I detest all my sins, because I dread the loss of heaven and the pains of hell. But most of all because I have offended You, my God, who are all good and deserving of all my love. I firmly resolve with the help of Your grace, to confess my sins, to do penance and to amend my life. Amen.

Step 8

Listen to the words of absolution and make a Sign of the Cross.

Step 9

If he closes by saying, "Give thanks to the Lord for He is good," answer, "For His mercy endures forever."

"The confession of evil works is the first beginning of good works."—St. Augustine

After Confession

Step 1   If you recall some serious sin you simply forgot to tell, don't worry, it has been forgiven with the others. Be sure to confess it next time you receive the Sacrament or Reconciliation.

Step 2   Do your assigned penance and resolve to return to the Sacrament of Reconciliation often.

Step 3   Thank God for the mercy and love He showered upon you in the Sacrament of Reconciliation; a simple, "Thank you God" or praying "The Glory Be" (Chapter 7) is sufficient.

Step 4   To preserve complete privacy, either destroy the worksheet that contains the list of your sins or make sure it does not fall into the hands of others.

"The confession of evil works is the first beginning of good works."—*St. Augustine*

CHAPTER 4

My Confession Worksheet

Today's Date: _____

Before Confession:

- Pray, "Come Holy Spirit" and make an Examination of Conscience. (Chapter 2)
- Pray for your confessor.

During Confession

- Priest welcomes you. Make the Sign of the Cross.
- Say **"Bless me Father, for I have sinned, this is my First Confession,"** or **"Bless me Father, for I have sinned, my last Confession was _____ (days, weeks, months) ago."**
- Tell the priest your sins below:

✔ The Lord says, "You Shall Love the Lord Your God with your whole heart."	# Of Times?
I did not obey God right away.	
I doubted God's love for me.	
I did not use all the graces God gave me to become closer to Him.	
I did not pray my daily prayers (morning, evening, meals).	
I put other things before God (friends, toys, games, and money).	
I did not try to do my best for Jesus, even when I had to do things I didn't want to.	
I spent money unwisely.	
I placed my faith things other than God (good luck charms, etc.)	
I said God's name in anger or frustration and / or spoke disrespectfully of God or Our Lady.	
I used bad words (swear words).	
I did not show reverence toward sacred persons, places, and things (e.g., the Pope, Bishop, priests, nuns, brothers, crucifixes, sacramentals, etc.).	
I missed Mass on purpose on a Sunday or Holy Day of Obligation.	
I was late for Mass or my behavior played a factor in our being late for Mass.	
I did not abstain or fast according to Church teaching (one hour before receiving Jesus in Eucharist, no meat on Friday during Lent, etc.).	
I laughed or distracted others in church.	
✔ The Lord Says, "You shall love your neighbor as yourself,"	
I did not give my parent, guardian, or teacher right-away obedience.	
I was disrespectful to my parent, guardian, or teacher.	

"The confession of evil works is the first beginning of good works."—St. Augustine

I did not do my chores without grumbling or needing to be nagged.	
I spoke uncharitably to my parent, guardian, teacher, friend, sibling, etc.	
I lied.	
I took something that did not belong to me.	
I teased someone.	
I hurt someone.	
I did not treat my body, a temple of the Holy Spirit, with respect (ate too much, dressed immodestly, avoided exercise, etc.).	
I did not respect other's personal space.	
I said unkind words to or about someone else.	
I became envious of something someone else has or has achieved.	
I became angry or envious and did not handle my feelings in a positive way.	
I was prideful or boastful.	
I could have helped somebody and chose not to.	
I could have shared and chose not to.	
I could have been charitable and chose not to.	

- Say, "**I am sorry for these and all of my sins**."
- Listen to the priest and pray an **Act of Contrition**:

  Act of Contrition - My God, I am sorry for my sins with all my heart. In choosing to do wrong and failing to do good, I have sinned against You whom I should love above all things. I firmly intend, with Your help, to do penance, to sin no more, and to avoid whatever leads me to sin. Our Savior Jesus Christ suffered and died for us. In His Name, my God, have mercy. Amen.

  Or

  Act of Contrition: O my God, I am heartily sorry for having offended You and I detest all my sins, because I dread the loss of heaven and the pains of hell. But most of all because I have offended You, my God, who are all good and deserving of all my love. I firmly resolve with the help of Your grace, to confess my sins, to do penance and to amend my life. Amen.

- Priest will say words of absolution (forgiveness). Make the Sign of the Cross.
- If he closes by saying, "Give thanks to the Lord for He is good," answer, **"For His mercy endures forever."**
- Perform your penance.
- Thank God.

"The confession of evil works is the first beginning of good works."—St. Augustine

Today's Date: _____

Before Confession:
- Pray, "Come Holy Spirit" and make an Examination of Conscience. (Chapter 2)
- Pray for your confessor.

During Confession
- Priest welcomes you. Make the Sign of the Cross.
- Say **"Bless me Father, for I have sinned, this is my First Confession,"** or **"Bless me Father, for I have sinned, my last Confession was** _____ **(days, weeks, months) ago."**
- Tell the priest your sins below:

✔	The Lord says, "You Shall Love the Lord Your God with your whole heart."	# Of Times?
	I did not obey God right away.	
	I doubted God's love for me.	
	I did not use all the graces God gave me to become closer to Him.	
	I did not pray my daily prayers (morning, evening, meals).	
	I put other things before God (friends, toys, games, and money).	
	I did not try to do my best for Jesus, even when I had to do things I didn't want to.	
	I spent money unwisely.	
	I placed my faith things other than God (good luck charms, etc.)	
	I said God's name in anger or frustration and / or spoke disrespectfully of God or Our Lady.	
	I used bad words (swear words).	
	I did not show reverence toward sacred persons, places, and things (e.g., the Pope, Bishop, priests, nuns, brothers, crucifixes, sacramentals, etc.).	
	I missed Mass on purpose on a Sunday or Holy Day of Obligation.	
	I was late for Mass or my behavior played a factor in our being late for Mass.	
	I did not abstain or fast according to Church teaching (one hour before receiving Jesus in Eucharist, no meat on Friday during Lent, etc.).	
	I laughed or distracted others in church.	
✔	The Lord Says, "You shall love your neighbor as yourself,"	
	I did not give my parent, guardian, or teacher right-away obedience.	
	I was disrespectful to my parent, guardian, or teacher.	

"The confession of evil works is the first beginning of good works."—St. Augustine

I did not do my chores without grumbling or needing to be nagged.	
I spoke uncharitably to my parent, guardian, teacher, friend, sibling, etc.	
I lied.	
I took something that did not belong to me.	
I teased someone.	
I hurt someone.	
I did not treat my body, a temple of the Holy Spirit, with respect (ate too much, dressed immodestly, avoided exercise, etc.).	
I did not respect other's personal space.	
I said unkind words to or about someone else.	
I became envious of something someone else has or has achieved.	
I became angry or envious and did not handle my feelings in a positive way.	
I was prideful or boastful.	
I could have helped somebody and chose not to.	
I could have shared and chose not to.	
I could have been charitable and chose not to.	

- Say, "**I am sorry for these and all of my sins.**"
- Listen to the priest and pray an **Act of Contrition**:

  Act of Contrition - My God, I am sorry for my sins with all my heart. In choosing to do wrong and failing to do good, I have sinned against You whom I should love above all things. I firmly intend, with Your help, to do penance, to sin no more, and to avoid whatever leads me to sin. Our Savior Jesus Christ suffered and died for us. In His Name, my God, have mercy. Amen.

  Or

  Act of Contrition: O my God, I am heartily sorry for having offended You and I detest all my sins, because I dread the loss of heaven and the pains of hell. But most of all because I have offended You, my God, who are all good and deserving of all my love. I firmly resolve with the help of Your grace, to confess my sins, to do penance and to amend my life. Amen.

- Priest will say words of absolution (forgiveness). Make the Sign of the Cross.
- If he closes by saying, "Give thanks to the Lord for He is good," answer, **"For His mercy endures forever."**
- Perform your penance.
- Thank God.

"The confession of evil works is the first beginning of good works."—St. Augustine

Today's Date: _____

Before Confession:

- Pray, "Come Holy Spirit" and make an Examination of Conscience. (Chapter 2)
- Pray for your confessor.

During Confession

- Priest welcomes you. Make the Sign of the Cross.
- Say "**Bless me Father, for I have sinned, this is my First Confession,**" or "**Bless me Father, for I have sinned, my last Confession was _____ (days, weeks, months) ago.**"
- Tell the priest your sins below:

✔ The Lord says, "You Shall Love the Lord Your God with your whole heart."	# Of Times?
I did not obey God right away.	
I doubted God's love for me.	
I did not use all the graces God gave me to become closer to Him.	
I did not pray my daily prayers (morning, evening, meals).	
I put other things before God (friends, toys, games, and money).	
I did not try to do my best for Jesus, even when I had to do things I didn't want to.	
I spent money unwisely.	
I placed my faith things other than God (good luck charms, etc.)	
I said God's name in anger or frustration and / or spoke disrespectfully of God or Our Lady.	
I used bad words (swear words).	
I did not show reverence toward sacred persons, places, and things (e.g., the Pope, Bishop, priests, nuns, brothers, crucifixes, sacramentals, etc.).	
I missed Mass on purpose on a Sunday or Holy Day of Obligation.	
I was late for Mass or my behavior played a factor in our being late for Mass.	
I did not abstain or fast according to Church teaching (one hour before receiving Jesus in Eucharist, no meat on Friday during Lent, etc.).	
I laughed or distracted others in church.	
✔ The Lord Says, "You shall love your neighbor as yourself,"	
I did not give my parent, guardian, or teacher right-away obedience.	
I was disrespectful to my parent, guardian, or teacher.	

"The confession of evil works is the first beginning of good works."—St. Augustine

I did not do my chores without grumbling or needing to be nagged.	
I spoke uncharitably to my parent, guardian, teacher, friend, sibling, etc.	
I lied.	
I took something that did not belong to me.	
I teased someone.	
I hurt someone.	
I did not treat my body, a temple of the Holy Spirit, with respect (ate too much, dressed immodestly, avoided exercise, etc.).	
I did not respect other's personal space.	
I said unkind words to or about someone else.	
I became envious of something someone else has or has achieved.	
I became angry or envious and did not handle my feelings in a positive way.	
I was prideful or boastful.	
I could have helped somebody and chose not to.	
I could have shared and chose not to.	
I could have been charitable and chose not to.	

- Say, "**I am sorry for these and all of my sins.**"
- Listen to the priest and pray an **Act of Contrition**:

  Act of Contrition - My God, I am sorry for my sins with all my heart. In choosing to do wrong and failing to do good, I have sinned against You whom I should love above all things. I firmly intend, with Your help, to do penance, to sin no more, and to avoid whatever leads me to sin. Our Savior Jesus Christ suffered and died for us. In His Name, my God, have mercy. Amen.

  Or

  Act of Contrition: O my God, I am heartily sorry for having offended You and I detest all my sins, because I dread the loss of heaven and the pains of hell. But most of all because I have offended You, my God, who are all good and deserving of all my love. I firmly resolve with the help of Your grace, to confess my sins, to do penance and to amend my life. Amen.

- Priest will say words of absolution (forgiveness). Make the Sign of the Cross.
- If he closes by saying, "Give thanks to the Lord for He is good," answer, **"For His mercy endures forever."**
- Perform your penance.
- Thank God.

"The confession of evil works is the first beginning of good works."—St. Augustine

Today's Date: _____

Before Confession:
- Pray, "Come Holy Spirit" and make an Examination of Conscience. (Chapter 2)
- Pray for your confessor.

During Confession
- Priest welcomes you. Make the Sign of the Cross.
- Say **"Bless me Father, for I have sinned, this is my First Confession,"** or **"Bless me Father, for I have sinned, my last Confession was _____ (days, weeks, months) ago."**
- Tell the priest your sins below:

✔ The Lord says, "You Shall Love the Lord Your God with your whole heart."	# Of Times?
I did not obey God right away.	
I doubted God's love for me.	
I did not use all the graces God gave me to become closer to Him.	
I did not pray my daily prayers (morning, evening, meals).	
I put other things before God (friends, toys, games, and money).	
I did not try to do my best for Jesus, even when I had to do things I didn't want to.	
I spent money unwisely.	
I placed my faith things other than God (good luck charms, etc.)	
I said God's name in anger or frustration and / or spoke disrespectfully of God or Our Lady.	
I used bad words (swear words).	
I did not show reverence toward sacred persons, places, and things (e.g., the Pope, Bishop, priests, nuns, brothers, crucifixes, sacramentals, etc.).	
I missed Mass on purpose on a Sunday or Holy Day of Obligation.	
I was late for Mass or my behavior played a factor in our being late for Mass.	
I did not abstain or fast according to Church teaching (one hour before receiving Jesus in Eucharist, no meat on Friday during Lent, etc.).	
I laughed or distracted others in church.	
✔ The Lord Says, "You shall love your neighbor as yourself,"	
I did not give my parent, guardian, or teacher right-away obedience.	
I was disrespectful to my parent, guardian, or teacher.	

"The confession of evil works is the first beginning of good works."—St. Augustine

I did not do my chores without grumbling or needing to be nagged.	
I spoke uncharitably to my parent, guardian, teacher, friend, sibling, etc.	
I lied.	
I took something that did not belong to me.	
I teased someone.	
I hurt someone.	
I did not treat my body, a temple of the Holy Spirit, with respect (ate too much, dressed immodestly, avoided exercise, etc.).	
I did not respect other's personal space.	
I said unkind words to or about someone else.	
I became envious of something someone else has or has achieved.	
I became angry or envious and did not handle my feelings in a positive way.	
I was prideful or boastful.	
I could have helped somebody and chose not to.	
I could have shared and chose not to.	
I could have been charitable and chose not to.	

- Say, "**I am sorry for these and all of my sins.**"
- Listen to the priest and pray an **Act of Contrition**:
  Act of Contrition - My God, I am sorry for my sins with all my heart. In choosing to do wrong and failing to do good, I have sinned against You whom I should love above all things. I firmly intend, with Your help, to do penance, to sin no more, and to avoid whatever leads me to sin. Our Savior Jesus Christ suffered and died for us. In His Name, my God, have mercy. Amen.
  Or
  Act of Contrition: O my God, I am heartily sorry for having offended You and I detest all my sins, because I dread the loss of heaven and the pains of hell. But most of all because I have offended You, my God, who are all good and deserving of all my love. I firmly resolve with the help of Your grace, to confess my sins, to do penance and to amend my life. Amen.

- Priest will say words of absolution (forgiveness). Make the Sign of the Cross.
- If he closes by saying, "Give thanks to the Lord for He is good," answer, "**For His mercy endures forever.**"
- Perform your penance.
- Thank God.

"The confession of evil works is the first beginning of good works."—*St. Augustine*

Today's Date: _____

Before Confession:

- Pray, "Come Holy Spirit" and make an Examination of Conscience. (Chapter 2)
- Pray for your confessor.

During Confession

- Priest welcomes you. Make the Sign of the Cross.
- Say "**Bless me Father, for I have sinned, this is my First Confession,**" or "**Bless me Father, for I have sinned, my last Confession was** _____ **(days, weeks, months) ago.**"
- Tell the priest your sins below:

✔	The Lord says, "You Shall Love the Lord Your God with your whole heart."	# Of Times?
	I did not obey God right away.	
	I doubted God's love for me.	
	I did not use all the graces God gave me to become closer to Him.	
	I did not pray my daily prayers (morning, evening, meals).	
	I put other things before God (friends, toys, games, and money).	
	I did not try to do my best for Jesus, even when I had to do things I didn't want to.	
	I spent money unwisely.	
	I placed my faith things other than God (good luck charms, etc.)	
	I said God's name in anger or frustration and / or spoke disrespectfully of God or Our Lady.	
	I used bad words (swear words).	
	I did not show reverence toward sacred persons, places, and things (e.g., the Pope, Bishop, priests, nuns, brothers, crucifixes, sacramentals, etc.).	
	I missed Mass on purpose on a Sunday or Holy Day of Obligation.	
	I was late for Mass or my behavior played a factor in our being late for Mass.	
	I did not abstain or fast according to Church teaching (one hour before receiving Jesus in Eucharist, no meat on Friday during Lent, etc.).	
	I laughed or distracted others in church.	
✔	The Lord Says, "You shall love your neighbor as yourself,"	
	I did not give my parent, guardian, or teacher right-away obedience.	
	I was disrespectful to my parent, guardian, or teacher.	

"The confession of evil works is the first beginning of good works."—St. Augustine

I did not do my chores without grumbling or needing to be nagged.	
I spoke uncharitably to my parent, guardian, teacher, friend, sibling, etc.	
I lied.	
I took something that did not belong to me.	
I teased someone.	
I hurt someone.	
I did not treat my body, a temple of the Holy Spirit, with respect (ate too much, dressed immodestly, avoided exercise, etc.).	
I did not respect other's personal space.	
I said unkind words to or about someone else.	
I became envious of something someone else has or has achieved.	
I became angry or envious and did not handle my feelings in a positive way.	
I was prideful or boastful.	
I could have helped somebody and chose not to.	
I could have shared and chose not to.	
I could have been charitable and chose not to.	

- Say, "**I am sorry for these and all of my sins**."
- Listen to the priest and pray an **Act of Contrition**:
  Act of Contrition - My God, I am sorry for my sins with all my heart. In choosing to do wrong and failing to do good, I have sinned against You whom I should love above all things. I firmly intend, with Your help, to do penance, to sin no more, and to avoid whatever leads me to sin. Our Savior Jesus Christ suffered and died for us. In His Name, my God, have mercy. Amen.
  Or
  Act of Contrition: O my God, I am heartily sorry for having offended You and I detest all my sins, because I dread the loss of heaven and the pains of hell. But most of all because I have offended You, my God, who are all good and deserving of all my love. I firmly resolve with the help of Your grace, to confess my sins, to do penance and to amend my life. Amen.

- Priest will say words of absolution (forgiveness). Make the Sign of the Cross.
- If he closes by saying, "Give thanks to the Lord for He is good," answer, **"For His mercy endures forever."**
- Perform your penance.
- Thank God.

"The confession of evil works is the first beginning of good works."—*St. Augustine*

Today's Date: _____

Before Confession:

- Pray, "Come Holy Spirit" and make an Examination of Conscience. (Chapter 2)
- Pray for your confessor.

During Confession

- Priest welcomes you. Make the Sign of the Cross.
- Say **"Bless me Father, for I have sinned, this is my First Confession,"** or **"Bless me Father, for I have sinned, my last Confession was _____ (days, weeks, months) ago."**
- Tell the priest your sins below:

✔	The Lord says, "You Shall Love the Lord Your God with your whole heart."	# Of Times?
	I did not obey God right away.	
	I doubted God's love for me.	
	I did not use all the graces God gave me to become closer to Him.	
	I did not pray my daily prayers (morning, evening, meals).	
	I put other things before God (friends, toys, games, and money).	
	I did not try to do my best for Jesus, even when I had to do things I didn't want to.	
	I spent money unwisely.	
	I placed my faith things other than God (good luck charms, etc.)	
	I said God's name in anger or frustration and / or spoke disrespectfully of God or Our Lady.	
	I used bad words (swear words).	
	I did not show reverence toward sacred persons, places, and things (e.g., the Pope, Bishop, priests, nuns, brothers, crucifixes, sacramentals, etc.).	
	I missed Mass on purpose on a Sunday or Holy Day of Obligation.	
	I was late for Mass or my behavior played a factor in our being late for Mass.	
	I did not abstain or fast according to Church teaching (one hour before receiving Jesus in Eucharist, no meat on Friday during Lent, etc.).	
	I laughed or distracted others in church.	
✔	The Lord Says, "You shall love your neighbor as yourself,"	
	I did not give my parent, guardian, or teacher right-away obedience.	
	I was disrespectful to my parent, guardian, or teacher.	

"The confession of evil works is the first beginning of good works."—St. Augustine

I did not do my chores without grumbling or needing to be nagged.	
I spoke uncharitably to my parent, guardian, teacher, friend, sibling, etc.	
I lied.	
I took something that did not belong to me.	
I teased someone.	
I hurt someone.	
I did not treat my body, a temple of the Holy Spirit, with respect (ate too much, dressed immodestly, avoided exercise, etc.).	
I did not respect other's personal space.	
I said unkind words to or about someone else.	
I became envious of something someone else has or has achieved.	
I became angry or envious and did not handle my feelings in a positive way.	
I was prideful or boastful.	
I could have helped somebody and chose not to.	
I could have shared and chose not to.	
I could have been charitable and chose not to.	

- Say, "**I am sorry for these and all of my sins.**"
- Listen to the priest and pray an **Act of Contrition**:
  Act of Contrition - My God, I am sorry for my sins with all my heart. In choosing to do wrong and failing to do good, I have sinned against You whom I should love above all things. I firmly intend, with Your help, to do penance, to sin no more, and to avoid whatever leads me to sin. Our Savior Jesus Christ suffered and died for us. In His Name, my God, have mercy. Amen.
  Or
  Act of Contrition: O my God, I am heartily sorry for having offended You and I detest all my sins, because I dread the loss of heaven and the pains of hell. But most of all because I have offended You, my God, who are all good and deserving of all my love. I firmly resolve with the help of Your grace, to confess my sins, to do penance and to amend my life. Amen.

- Priest will say words of absolution (forgiveness). Make the Sign of the Cross.
- If he closes by saying, "Give thanks to the Lord for He is good," answer, **"For His mercy endures forever."**
- Perform your penance.
- Thank God.

"The confession of evil works is the first beginning of good works."—St. Augustine

Today's Date: _____

Before Confession:

- Pray, "Come Holy Spirit" and make an Examination of Conscience. (Chapter 2)
- Pray for your confessor.

During Confession

- Priest welcomes you. Make the Sign of the Cross.
- Say "**Bless me Father, for I have sinned, this is my First Confession**," or "**Bless me Father, for I have sinned, my last Confession was _____ (days, weeks, months) ago.**"
- Tell the priest your sins below:

✔	The Lord says, "You Shall Love the Lord Your God with your whole heart."	# Of Times?
	I did not obey God right away.	
	I doubted God's love for me.	
	I did not use all the graces God gave me to become closer to Him.	
	I did not pray my daily prayers (morning, evening, meals).	
	I put other things before God (friends, toys, games, and money).	
	I did not try to do my best for Jesus, even when I had to do things I didn't want to.	
	I spent money unwisely.	
	I placed my faith things other than God (good luck charms, etc.)	
	I said God's name in anger or frustration and / or spoke disrespectfully of God or Our Lady.	
	I used bad words (swear words).	
	I did not show reverence toward sacred persons, places, and things (e.g., the Pope, Bishop, priests, nuns, brothers, crucifixes, sacramentals, etc.).	
	I missed Mass on purpose on a Sunday or Holy Day of Obligation.	
	I was late for Mass or my behavior played a factor in our being late for Mass.	
	I did not abstain or fast according to Church teaching (one hour before receiving Jesus in Eucharist, no meat on Friday during Lent, etc.).	
	I laughed or distracted others in church.	
✔	The Lord Says, "You shall love your neighbor as yourself."	
	I did not give my parent, guardian, or teacher right-away obedience.	
	I was disrespectful to my parent, guardian, or teacher.	

"The confession of evil works is the first beginning of good works."—St. Augustine

I did not do my chores without grumbling or needing to be nagged.	
I spoke uncharitably to my parent, guardian, teacher, friend, sibling, etc.	
I lied.	
I took something that did not belong to me.	
I teased someone.	
I hurt someone.	
I did not treat my body, a temple of the Holy Spirit, with respect (ate too much, dressed immodestly, avoided exercise, etc.).	
I did not respect other's personal space.	
I said unkind words to or about someone else.	
I became envious of something someone else has or has achieved.	
I became angry or envious and did not handle my feelings in a positive way.	
I was prideful or boastful.	
I could have helped somebody and chose not to.	
I could have shared and chose not to.	
I could have been charitable and chose not to.	

- Say, "**I am sorry for these and all of my sins.**"
- Listen to the priest and pray an **Act of Contrition**:

  Act of Contrition - My God, I am sorry for my sins with all my heart. In choosing to do wrong and failing to do good, I have sinned against You whom I should love above all things. I firmly intend, with Your help, to do penance, to sin no more, and to avoid whatever leads me to sin. Our Savior Jesus Christ suffered and died for us. In His Name, my God, have mercy. Amen.

  Or

  Act of Contrition: O my God, I am heartily sorry for having offended You and I detest all my sins, because I dread the loss of heaven and the pains of hell. But most of all because I have offended You, my God, who are all good and deserving of all my love. I firmly resolve with the help of Your grace, to confess my sins, to do penance and to amend my life. Amen.

- Priest will say words of absolution (forgiveness). Make the Sign of the Cross.
- If he closes by saying, "Give thanks to the Lord for He is good," answer, **"For His mercy endures forever."**
- Perform your penance.
- Thank God.

"The confession of evil works is the first beginning of good works."—St. Augustine

Today's Date: _____

Before Confession:
- Pray, "Come Holy Spirit" and make an Examination of Conscience. (Chapter 2)
- Pray for your confessor.

During Confession
- Priest welcomes you. Make the Sign of the Cross.
- Say "**Bless me Father, for I have sinned, this is my First Confession,**" or "**Bless me Father, for I have sinned, my last Confession was** _____ **(days, weeks, months) ago.**"
- Tell the priest your sins below:

✔	The Lord says, "You Shall Love the Lord Your God with your whole heart."	# Of Times?
	I did not obey God right away.	
	I doubted God's love for me.	
	I did not use all the graces God gave me to become closer to Him.	
	I did not pray my daily prayers (morning, evening, meals).	
	I put other things before God (friends, toys, games, and money).	
	I did not try to do my best for Jesus, even when I had to do things I didn't want to.	
	I spent money unwisely.	
	I placed my faith things other than God (good luck charms, etc.)	
	I said God's name in anger or frustration and / or spoke disrespectfully of God or Our Lady.	
	I used bad words (swear words).	
	I did not show reverence toward sacred persons, places, and things (e.g., the Pope, Bishop, priests, nuns, brothers, crucifixes, sacramentals, etc.).	
	I missed Mass on purpose on a Sunday or Holy Day of Obligation.	
	I was late for Mass or my behavior played a factor in our being late for Mass.	
	I did not abstain or fast according to Church teaching (one hour before receiving Jesus in Eucharist, no meat on Friday during Lent, etc.).	
	I laughed or distracted others in church.	
✔	The Lord Says, "You shall love your neighbor as yourself,"	
	I did not give my parent, guardian, or teacher right-away obedience.	
	I was disrespectful to my parent, guardian, or teacher.	

"The confession of evil works is the first beginning of good works."—*St. Augustine*

I did not do my chores without grumbling or needing to be nagged.	
I spoke uncharitably to my parent, guardian, teacher, friend, sibling, etc.	
I lied.	
I took something that did not belong to me.	
I teased someone.	
I hurt someone.	
I did not treat my body, a temple of the Holy Spirit, with respect (ate too much, dressed immodestly, avoided exercise, etc.).	
I did not respect other's personal space.	
I said unkind words to or about someone else.	
I became envious of something someone else has or has achieved.	
I became angry or envious and did not handle my feelings in a positive way.	
I was prideful or boastful.	
I could have helped somebody and chose not to.	
I could have shared and chose not to.	
I could have been charitable and chose not to.	

- Say, "**I am sorry for these and all of my sins.**"
- Listen to the priest and pray an **Act of Contrition**:
  Act of Contrition - My God, I am sorry for my sins with all my heart. In choosing to do wrong and failing to do good, I have sinned against You whom I should love above all things. I firmly intend, with Your help, to do penance, to sin no more, and to avoid whatever leads me to sin. Our Savior Jesus Christ suffered and died for us. In His Name, my God, have mercy. Amen.
  Or
  Act of Contrition: O my God, I am heartily sorry for having offended You and I detest all my sins, because I dread the loss of heaven and the pains of hell. But most of all because I have offended You, my God, who are all good and deserving of all my love. I firmly resolve with the help of Your grace, to confess my sins, to do penance and to amend my life. Amen.

- Priest will say words of absolution (forgiveness). Make the Sign of the Cross.
- If he closes by saying, "Give thanks to the Lord for He is good," answer, **"For His mercy endures forever."**
- Perform your penance.
- Thank God.

"The confession of evil works is the first beginning of good works."—St. Augustine

Today's Date: _____

Before Confession:
- Pray, "Come Holy Spirit" and make an Examination of Conscience. (Chapter 2)
- Pray for your confessor.

During Confession
- Priest welcomes you. Make the Sign of the Cross.
- Say "**Bless me Father, for I have sinned, this is my First Confession,**" or "**Bless me Father, for I have sinned, my last Confession was _____ (days, weeks, months) ago.**"
- Tell the priest your sins below:

✔ The Lord says, "You Shall Love the Lord Your God with your whole heart."	# Of Times?
I did not obey God right away.	
I doubted God's love for me.	
I did not use all the graces God gave me to become closer to Him.	
I did not pray my daily prayers (morning, evening, meals).	
I put other things before God (friends, toys, games, and money).	
I did not try to do my best for Jesus, even when I had to do things I didn't want to.	
I spent money unwisely.	
I placed my faith things other than God (good luck charms, etc.)	
I said God's name in anger or frustration and / or spoke disrespectfully of God or Our Lady.	
I used bad words (swear words).	
I did not show reverence toward sacred persons, places, and things (e.g., the Pope, Bishop, priests, nuns, brothers, crucifixes, sacramentals, etc.).	
I missed Mass on purpose on a Sunday or Holy Day of Obligation.	
I was late for Mass or my behavior played a factor in our being late for Mass.	
I did not abstain or fast according to Church teaching (one hour before receiving Jesus in Eucharist, no meat on Friday during Lent, etc.).	
I laughed or distracted others in church.	
✔ The Lord Says, "You shall love your neighbor as yourself,"	
I did not give my parent, guardian, or teacher right-away obedience.	
I was disrespectful to my parent, guardian, or teacher.	

"The confession of evil works is the first beginning of good works."—St. Augustine

I did not do my chores without grumbling or needing to be nagged.	
I spoke uncharitably to my parent, guardian, teacher, friend, sibling, etc.	
I lied.	
I took something that did not belong to me.	
I teased someone.	
I hurt someone.	
I did not treat my body, a temple of the Holy Spirit, with respect (ate too much, dressed immodestly, avoided exercise, etc.).	
I did not respect other's personal space.	
I said unkind words to or about someone else.	
I became envious of something someone else has or has achieved.	
I became angry or envious and did not handle my feelings in a positive way.	
I was prideful or boastful.	
I could have helped somebody and chose not to.	
I could have shared and chose not to.	
I could have been charitable and chose not to.	

- Say, "**I am sorry for these and all of my sins.**"
- Listen to the priest and pray an **Act of Contrition**:
  Act of Contrition - My God, I am sorry for my sins with all my heart. In choosing to do wrong and failing to do good, I have sinned against You whom I should love above all things. I firmly intend, with Your help, to do penance, to sin no more, and to avoid whatever leads me to sin. Our Savior Jesus Christ suffered and died for us. In His Name, my God, have mercy. Amen.
  Or
  Act of Contrition: O my God, I am heartily sorry for having offended You and I detest all my sins, because I dread the loss of heaven and the pains of hell. But most of all because I have offended You, my God, who are all good and deserving of all my love. I firmly resolve with the help of Your grace, to confess my sins, to do penance and to amend my life. Amen.

- Priest will say words of absolution (forgiveness). Make the Sign of the Cross.
- If he closes by saying, "Give thanks to the Lord for He is good," answer, "**For His mercy endures forever.**"
- Perform your penance.
- Thank God.

"The confession of evil works is the first beginning of good works."—St. Augustine

Today's Date: _____

Before Confession:

- Pray, "Come Holy Spirit" and make an Examination of Conscience. (Chapter 2)
- Pray for your confessor.

During Confession

- Priest welcomes you. Make the Sign of the Cross.
- Say **"Bless me Father, for I have sinned, this is my First Confession,"** or **"Bless me Father, for I have sinned, my last Confession was _____ (days, weeks, months) ago."**
- Tell the priest your sins below:

✔	The Lord says, "You Shall Love the Lord Your God with your whole heart."	# Of Times?
	I did not obey God right away.	
	I doubted God's love for me.	
	I did not use all the graces God gave me to become closer to Him.	
	I did not pray my daily prayers (morning, evening, meals).	
	I put other things before God (friends, toys, games, and money).	
	I did not try to do my best for Jesus, even when I had to do things I didn't want to.	
	I spent money unwisely.	
	I placed my faith things other than God (good luck charms, etc.)	
	I said God's name in anger or frustration and / or spoke disrespectfully of God or Our Lady.	
	I used bad words (swear words).	
	I did not show reverence toward sacred persons, places, and things (e.g., the Pope, Bishop, priests, nuns, brothers, crucifixes, sacramentals, etc.).	
	I missed Mass on purpose on a Sunday or Holy Day of Obligation.	
	I was late for Mass or my behavior played a factor in our being late for Mass.	
	I did not abstain or fast according to Church teaching (one hour before receiving Jesus in Eucharist, no meat on Friday during Lent, etc.).	
	I laughed or distracted others in church.	
✔	The Lord Says, "You shall love your neighbor as yourself,"	
	I did not give my parent, guardian, or teacher right-away obedience.	
	I was disrespectful to my parent, guardian, or teacher.	

"The confession of evil works is the first beginning of good works."—St. Augustine

I did not do my chores without grumbling or needing to be nagged.	
I spoke uncharitably to my parent, guardian, teacher, friend, sibling, etc.	
I lied.	
I took something that did not belong to me.	
I teased someone.	
I hurt someone.	
I did not treat my body, a temple of the Holy Spirit, with respect (ate too much, dressed immodestly, avoided exercise, etc.).	
I did not respect other's personal space.	
I said unkind words to or about someone else.	
I became envious of something someone else has or has achieved.	
I became angry or envious and did not handle my feelings in a positive way.	
I was prideful or boastful.	
I could have helped somebody and chose not to.	
I could have shared and chose not to.	
I could have been charitable and chose not to.	

- Say, "**I am sorry for these and all of my sins.**"
- Listen to the priest and pray an **Act of Contrition**:
  Act of Contrition - My God, I am sorry for my sins with all my heart. In choosing to do wrong and failing to do good, I have sinned against You whom I should love above all things. I firmly intend, with Your help, to do penance, to sin no more, and to avoid whatever leads me to sin. Our Savior Jesus Christ suffered and died for us. In His Name, my God, have mercy. Amen.
  Or
  Act of Contrition: O my God, I am heartily sorry for having offended You and I detest all my sins, because I dread the loss of heaven and the pains of hell. But most of all because I have offended You, my God, who are all good and deserving of all my love. I firmly resolve with the help of Your grace, to confess my sins, to do penance and to amend my life. Amen.

- Priest will say words of absolution (forgiveness). Make the Sign of the Cross.
- If he closes by saying, "Give thanks to the Lord for He is good," answer, **"For His mercy endures forever."**
- Perform your penance.
- Thank God.

"The confession of evil works is the first beginning of good works."—*St. Augustine*

Today's Date: _____

Before Confession:
- Pray, "Come Holy Spirit" and make an Examination of Conscience. (Chapter 2)
- Pray for your confessor.

During Confession
- Priest welcomes you. Make the Sign of the Cross.
- Say **"Bless me Father, for I have sinned, this is my First Confession,"** or **"Bless me Father, for I have sinned, my last Confession was _____ (days, weeks, months) ago."**
- Tell the priest your sins below:

✔ The Lord says, "You Shall Love the Lord Your God with your whole heart."	# Of Times?
I did not obey God right away.	
I doubted God's love for me.	
I did not use all the graces God gave me to become closer to Him.	
I did not pray my daily prayers (morning, evening, meals).	
I put other things before God (friends, toys, games, and money).	
I did not try to do my best for Jesus, even when I had to do things I didn't want to.	
I spent money unwisely.	
I placed my faith things other than God (good luck charms, etc.)	
I said God's name in anger or frustration and / or spoke disrespectfully of God or Our Lady.	
I used bad words (swear words).	
I did not show reverence toward sacred persons, places, and things (e.g., the Pope, Bishop, priests, nuns, brothers, crucifixes, sacramentals, etc.).	
I missed Mass on purpose on a Sunday or Holy Day of Obligation.	
I was late for Mass or my behavior played a factor in our being late for Mass.	
I did not abstain or fast according to Church teaching (one hour before receiving Jesus in Eucharist, no meat on Friday during Lent, etc.).	
I laughed or distracted others in church.	
✔ The Lord Says, "You shall love your neighbor as yourself,"	
I did not give my parent, guardian, or teacher right-away obedience.	
I was disrespectful to my parent, guardian, or teacher.	

"The confession of evil works is the first beginning of good works."—St. Augustine

I did not do my chores without grumbling or needing to be nagged.	
I spoke uncharitably to my parent, guardian, teacher, friend, sibling, etc.	
I lied.	
I took something that did not belong to me.	
I teased someone.	
I hurt someone.	
I did not treat my body, a temple of the Holy Spirit, with respect (ate too much, dressed immodestly, avoided exercise, etc.).	
I did not respect other's personal space.	
I said unkind words to or about someone else.	
I became envious of something someone else has or has achieved.	
I became angry or envious and did not handle my feelings in a positive way.	
I was prideful or boastful.	
I could have helped somebody and chose not to.	
I could have shared and chose not to.	
I could have been charitable and chose not to.	

- Say, "**I am sorry for these and all of my sins.**"
- Listen to the priest and pray an **Act of Contrition**:
  Act of Contrition - My God, I am sorry for my sins with all my heart. In choosing to do wrong and failing to do good, I have sinned against You whom I should love above all things. I firmly intend, with Your help, to do penance, to sin no more, and to avoid whatever leads me to sin. Our Savior Jesus Christ suffered and died for us. In His Name, my God, have mercy. Amen.
  Or
  Act of Contrition: O my God, I am heartily sorry for having offended You and I detest all my sins, because I dread the loss of heaven and the pains of hell. But most of all because I have offended You, my God, who are all good and deserving of all my love. I firmly resolve with the help of Your grace, to confess my sins, to do penance and to amend my life. Amen.

- Priest will say words of absolution (forgiveness). Make the Sign of the Cross.
- If he closes by saying, "Give thanks to the Lord for He is good," answer, "**For His mercy endures forever.**"
- Perform your penance.
- Thank God.

"The confession of evil works is the first beginning of good works."—St. Augustine

Today's Date: _____

Before Confession:

- Pray, "Come Holy Spirit" and make an Examination of Conscience. (Chapter 2)
- Pray for your confessor.

During Confession

- Priest welcomes you. Make the Sign of the Cross.
- Say **"Bless me Father, for I have sinned, this is my First Confession,"** or **"Bless me Father, for I have sinned, my last Confession was _____ (days, weeks, months) ago."**
- Tell the priest your sins below:

✔	The Lord says, "You Shall Love the Lord Your God with your whole heart."	# Of Times?
	I did not obey God right away.	
	I doubted God's love for me.	
	I did not use all the graces God gave me to become closer to Him.	
	I did not pray my daily prayers (morning, evening, meals).	
	I put other things before God (friends, toys, games, and money).	
	I did not try to do my best for Jesus, even when I had to do things I didn't want to.	
	I spent money unwisely.	
	I placed my faith things other than God (good luck charms, etc.)	
	I said God's name in anger or frustration and / or spoke disrespectfully of God or Our Lady.	
	I used bad words (swear words).	
	I did not show reverence toward sacred persons, places, and things (e.g., the Pope, Bishop, priests, nuns, brothers, crucifixes, sacramentals, etc.).	
	I missed Mass on purpose on a Sunday or Holy Day of Obligation.	
	I was late for Mass or my behavior played a factor in our being late for Mass.	
	I did not abstain or fast according to Church teaching (one hour before receiving Jesus in Eucharist, no meat on Friday during Lent, etc.).	
	I laughed or distracted others in church.	
✔	The Lord Says, "You shall love your neighbor as yourself,"	
	I did not give my parent, guardian, or teacher right-away obedience.	
	I was disrespectful to my parent, guardian, or teacher.	

"The confession of evil works is the first beginning of good works."—St. Augustine

I did not do my chores without grumbling or needing to be nagged.	
I spoke uncharitably to my parent, guardian, teacher, friend, sibling, etc.	
I lied.	
I took something that did not belong to me.	
I teased someone.	
I hurt someone.	
I did not treat my body, a temple of the Holy Spirit, with respect (ate too much, dressed immodestly, avoided exercise, etc.).	
I did not respect other's personal space.	
I said unkind words to or about someone else.	
I became envious of something someone else has or has achieved.	
I became angry or envious and did not handle my feelings in a positive way.	
I was prideful or boastful.	
I could have helped somebody and chose not to.	
I could have shared and chose not to.	
I could have been charitable and chose not to.	

- Say, "**I am sorry for these and all of my sins.**"
- Listen to the priest and pray an **Act of Contrition**:
  Act of Contrition - My God, I am sorry for my sins with all my heart. In choosing to do wrong and failing to do good, I have sinned against You whom I should love above all things. I firmly intend, with Your help, to do penance, to sin no more, and to avoid whatever leads me to sin. Our Savior Jesus Christ suffered and died for us. In His Name, my God, have mercy. Amen.
  Or
  Act of Contrition: O my God, I am heartily sorry for having offended You and I detest all my sins, because I dread the loss of heaven and the pains of hell. But most of all because I have offended You, my God, who are all good and deserving of all my love. I firmly resolve with the help of Your grace, to confess my sins, to do penance and to amend my life. Amen.

- Priest will say words of absolution (forgiveness). Make the Sign of the Cross.
- If he closes by saying, "Give thanks to the Lord for He is good," answer, **"For His mercy endures forever."**
- Perform your penance.
- Thank God.

"The confession of evil works is the first beginning of good works."—St. Augustine

Today's Date: _____

Before Confession:

- Pray, "Come Holy Spirit" and make an Examination of Conscience. (Chapter 2)
- Pray for your confessor.

During Confession

- Priest welcomes you. Make the Sign of the Cross.
- Say "**Bless me Father, for I have sinned, this is my First Confession,**" or "**Bless me Father, for I have sinned, my last Confession was** _____ (days, weeks, months) ago.**"
- Tell the priest your sins below:

✔	The Lord says, "You Shall Love the Lord Your God with your whole heart."	# Of Times?
	I did not obey God right away.	
	I doubted God's love for me.	
	I did not use all the graces God gave me to become closer to Him.	
	I did not pray my daily prayers (morning, evening, meals).	
	I put other things before God (friends, toys, games, and money).	
	I did not try to do my best for Jesus, even when I had to do things I didn't want to.	
	I spent money unwisely.	
	I placed my faith things other than God (good luck charms, etc.)	
	I said God's name in anger or frustration and / or spoke disrespectfully of God or Our Lady.	
	I used bad words (swear words).	
	I did not show reverence toward sacred persons, places, and things (e.g., the Pope, Bishop, priests, nuns, brothers, crucifixes, sacramentals, etc.).	
	I missed Mass on purpose on a Sunday or Holy Day of Obligation.	
	I was late for Mass or my behavior played a factor in our being late for Mass.	
	I did not abstain or fast according to Church teaching (one hour before receiving Jesus in Eucharist, no meat on Friday during Lent, etc.).	
	I laughed or distracted others in church.	
✔	The Lord Says, "You shall love your neighbor as yourself,"	
	I did not give my parent, guardian, or teacher right-away obedience.	
	I was disrespectful to my parent, guardian, or teacher.	

"The confession of evil works is the first beginning of good works."—St. Augustine

I did not do my chores without grumbling or needing to be nagged.		
I spoke uncharitably to my parent, guardian, teacher, friend, sibling, etc.		
I lied.		
I took something that did not belong to me.		
I teased someone.		
I hurt someone.		
I did not treat my body, a temple of the Holy Spirit, with respect (ate too much, dressed immodestly, avoided exercise, etc.).		
I did not respect other's personal space.		
I said unkind words to or about someone else.		
I became envious of something someone else has or has achieved.		
I became angry or envious and did not handle my feelings in a positive way.		
I was prideful or boastful.		
I could have helped somebody and chose not to.		
I could have shared and chose not to.		
I could have been charitable and chose not to.		

- Say, "**I am sorry for these and all of my sins.**"
- Listen to the priest and pray an **Act of Contrition**:
  Act of Contrition - My God, I am sorry for my sins with all my heart. In choosing to do wrong and failing to do good, I have sinned against You whom I should love above all things. I firmly intend, with Your help, to do penance, to sin no more, and to avoid whatever leads me to sin. Our Savior Jesus Christ suffered and died for us. In His Name, my God, have mercy. Amen.
  Or
  Act of Contrition: O my God, I am heartily sorry for having offended You and I detest all my sins, because I dread the loss of heaven and the pains of hell. But most of all because I have offended You, my God, who are all good and deserving of all my love. I firmly resolve with the help of Your grace, to confess my sins, to do penance and to amend my life. Amen.

- Priest will say words of absolution (forgiveness). Make the Sign of the Cross.
- If he closes by saying, "Give thanks to the Lord for He is good," answer, "**For His mercy endures forever.**"
- Perform your penance.
- Thank God.

"The confession of evil works is the first beginning of good works."—St. Augustine

Today's Date: _____

Before Confession:
- Pray, "Come Holy Spirit" and make an Examination of Conscience. (Chapter 2)
- Pray for your confessor.

During Confession
- Priest welcomes you. Make the Sign of the Cross.
- Say "**Bless me Father, for I have sinned, this is my First Confession,**" or "**Bless me Father, for I have sinned, my last Confession was _____ (days, weeks, months) ago.**"
- Tell the priest your sins below:

✔	The Lord says, "You Shall Love the Lord Your God with your whole heart."	# Of Times?
	I did not obey God right away.	
	I doubted God's love for me.	
	I did not use all the graces God gave me to become closer to Him.	
	I did not pray my daily prayers (morning, evening, meals).	
	I put other things before God (friends, toys, games, and money).	
	I did not try to do my best for Jesus, even when I had to do things I didn't want to.	
	I spent money unwisely.	
	I placed my faith things other than God (good luck charms, etc.)	
	I said God's name in anger or frustration and / or spoke disrespectfully of God or Our Lady.	
	I used bad words (swear words).	
	I did not show reverence toward sacred persons, places, and things (e.g., the Pope, Bishop, priests, nuns, brothers, crucifixes, sacramentals, etc.).	
	I missed Mass on purpose on a Sunday or Holy Day of Obligation.	
	I was late for Mass or my behavior played a factor in our being late for Mass.	
	I did not abstain or fast according to Church teaching (one hour before receiving Jesus in Eucharist, no meat on Friday during Lent, etc.).	
	I laughed or distracted others in church.	
✔	The Lord Says, "You shall love your neighbor as yourself,"	
	I did not give my parent, guardian, or teacher right-away obedience.	
	I was disrespectful to my parent, guardian, or teacher.	

"The confession of evil works is the first beginning of good works."—St. Augustine

I did not do my chores without grumbling or needing to be nagged.	
I spoke uncharitably to my parent, guardian, teacher, friend, sibling, etc.	
I lied.	
I took something that did not belong to me.	
I teased someone.	
I hurt someone.	
I did not treat my body, a temple of the Holy Spirit, with respect (ate too much, dressed immodestly, avoided exercise, etc.).	
I did not respect other's personal space.	
I said unkind words to or about someone else.	
I became envious of something someone else has or has achieved.	
I became angry or envious and did not handle my feelings in a positive way.	
I was prideful or boastful.	
I could have helped somebody and chose not to.	
I could have shared and chose not to.	
I could have been charitable and chose not to.	

- Say, "**I am sorry for these and all of my sins.**"
- Listen to the priest and pray an **Act of Contrition**:
  Act of Contrition - My God, I am sorry for my sins with all my heart. In choosing to do wrong and failing to do good, I have sinned against You whom I should love above all things. I firmly intend, with Your help, to do penance, to sin no more, and to avoid whatever leads me to sin. Our Savior Jesus Christ suffered and died for us. In His Name, my God, have mercy. Amen.
  Or
  Act of Contrition: O my God, I am heartily sorry for having offended You and I detest all my sins, because I dread the loss of heaven and the pains of hell. But most of all because I have offended You, my God, who are all good and deserving of all my love. I firmly resolve with the help of Your grace, to confess my sins, to do penance and to amend my life. Amen.

- Priest will say words of absolution (forgiveness). Make the Sign of the Cross.
- If he closes by saying, "Give thanks to the Lord for He is good," answer, "**For His mercy endures forever.**"
- Perform your penance.
- Thank God.

"The confession of evil works is the first beginning of good works."—St. Augustine

Today's Date: _____

Before Confession:

- Pray, "Come Holy Spirit" and make an Examination of Conscience. (Chapter 2)
- Pray for your confessor.

During Confession

- Priest welcomes you. Make the Sign of the Cross.
- Say **"Bless me Father, for I have sinned, this is my First Confession,"** or **"Bless me Father, for I have sinned, my last Confession was _____ (days, weeks, months) ago."**
- Tell the priest your sins below:

✔	The Lord says, "You Shall Love the Lord Your God with your whole heart."	# Of Times?
	I did not obey God right away.	
	I doubted God's love for me.	
	I did not use all the graces God gave me to become closer to Him.	
	I did not pray my daily prayers (morning, evening, meals).	
	I put other things before God (friends, toys, games, and money).	
	I did not try to do my best for Jesus, even when I had to do things I didn't want to.	
	I spent money unwisely.	
	I placed my faith things other than God (good luck charms, etc.)	
	I said God's name in anger or frustration and / or spoke disrespectfully of God or Our Lady.	
	I used bad words (swear words).	
	I did not show reverence toward sacred persons, places, and things (e.g., the Pope, Bishop, priests, nuns, brothers, crucifixes, sacramentals, etc.).	
	I missed Mass on purpose on a Sunday or Holy Day of Obligation.	
	I was late for Mass or my behavior played a factor in our being late for Mass.	
	I did not abstain or fast according to Church teaching (one hour before receiving Jesus in Eucharist, no meat on Friday during Lent, etc.).	
	I laughed or distracted others in church.	
✔	The Lord Says, "You shall love your neighbor as yourself,"	
	I did not give my parent, guardian, or teacher right-away obedience.	
	I was disrespectful to my parent, guardian, or teacher.	

"The confession of evil works is the first beginning of good works."—St. Augustine

I did not do my chores without grumbling or needing to be nagged.	
I spoke uncharitably to my parent, guardian, teacher, friend, sibling, etc.	
I lied.	
I took something that did not belong to me.	
I teased someone.	
I hurt someone.	
I did not treat my body, a temple of the Holy Spirit, with respect (ate too much, dressed immodestly, avoided exercise, etc.).	
I did not respect other's personal space.	
I said unkind words to or about someone else.	
I became envious of something someone else has or has achieved.	
I became angry or envious and did not handle my feelings in a positive way.	
I was prideful or boastful.	
I could have helped somebody and chose not to.	
I could have shared and chose not to.	
I could have been charitable and chose not to.	

- Say, "**I am sorry for these and all of my sins.**"
- Listen to the priest and pray an **Act of Contrition**:
  Act of Contrition - My God, I am sorry for my sins with all my heart. In choosing to do wrong and failing to do good, I have sinned against You whom I should love above all things. I firmly intend, with Your help, to do penance, to sin no more, and to avoid whatever leads me to sin. Our Savior Jesus Christ suffered and died for us. In His Name, my God, have mercy. Amen.
  Or
  Act of Contrition: O my God, I am heartily sorry for having offended You and I detest all my sins, because I dread the loss of heaven and the pains of hell. But most of all because I have offended You, my God, who are all good and deserving of all my love. I firmly resolve with the help of Your grace, to confess my sins, to do penance and to amend my life. Amen.

- Priest will say words of absolution (forgiveness). Make the Sign of the Cross.
- If he closes by saying, "Give thanks to the Lord for He is good," answer, **"For His mercy endures forever."**
- Perform your penance.
- Thank God.

"The confession of evil works is the first beginning of good works."—St. Augustine

Today's Date: _____

Before Confession:
- Pray, "Come Holy Spirit" and make an Examination of Conscience. (Chapter 2)
- Pray for your confessor.

During Confession
- Priest welcomes you. Make the Sign of the Cross.
- Say **"Bless me Father, for I have sinned, this is my First Confession,"** or **"Bless me Father, for I have sinned, my last Confession was _____ (days, weeks, months) ago."**
- Tell the priest your sins below:

✔	The Lord says, "You Shall Love the Lord Your God with your whole heart."	# Of Times?
	I did not obey God right away.	
	I doubted God's love for me.	
	I did not use all the graces God gave me to become closer to Him.	
	I did not pray my daily prayers (morning, evening, meals).	
	I put other things before God (friends, toys, games, and money).	
	I did not try to do my best for Jesus, even when I had to do things I didn't want to.	
	I spent money unwisely.	
	I placed my faith things other than God (good luck charms, etc.)	
	I said God's name in anger or frustration and / or spoke disrespectfully of God or Our Lady.	
	I used bad words (swear words).	
	I did not show reverence toward sacred persons, places, and things (e.g., the Pope, Bishop, priests, nuns, brothers, crucifixes, sacramentals, etc.).	
	I missed Mass on purpose on a Sunday or Holy Day of Obligation.	
	I was late for Mass or my behavior played a factor in our being late for Mass.	
	I did not abstain or fast according to Church teaching (one hour before receiving Jesus in Eucharist, no meat on Friday during Lent, etc.).	
	I laughed or distracted others in church.	
✔	The Lord Says, "You shall love your neighbor as yourself,"	
	I did not give my parent, guardian, or teacher right-away obedience.	
	I was disrespectful to my parent, guardian, or teacher.	

"The confession of evil works is the first beginning of good works."—St. Augustine

I did not do my chores without grumbling or needing to be nagged.	
I spoke uncharitably to my parent, guardian, teacher, friend, sibling, etc.	
I lied.	
I took something that did not belong to me.	
I teased someone.	
I hurt someone.	
I did not treat my body, a temple of the Holy Spirit, with respect (ate too much, dressed immodestly, avoided exercise, etc.).	
I did not respect other's personal space.	
I said unkind words to or about someone else.	
I became envious of something someone else has or has achieved.	
I became angry or envious and did not handle my feelings in a positive way.	
I was prideful or boastful.	
I could have helped somebody and chose not to.	
I could have shared and chose not to.	
I could have been charitable and chose not to.	

- Say, "**I am sorry for these and all of my sins.**"
- Listen to the priest and pray an **Act of Contrition**:
  Act of Contrition - My God, I am sorry for my sins with all my heart. In choosing to do wrong and failing to do good, I have sinned against You whom I should love above all things. I firmly intend, with Your help, to do penance, to sin no more, and to avoid whatever leads me to sin. Our Savior Jesus Christ suffered and died for us. In His Name, my God, have mercy. Amen.
  Or
  Act of Contrition: O my God, I am heartily sorry for having offended You and I detest all my sins, because I dread the loss of heaven and the pains of hell. But most of all because I have offended You, my God, who are all good and deserving of all my love. I firmly resolve with the help of Your grace, to confess my sins, to do penance and to amend my life. Amen.

- Priest will say words of absolution (forgiveness). Make the Sign of the Cross.
- If he closes by saying, "Give thanks to the Lord for He is good," answer, **"For His mercy endures forever."**
- Perform your penance.
- Thank God.

"The confession of evil works is the first beginning of good works."—St. Augustine

Today's Date: _____

Before Confession:
- Pray, "Come Holy Spirit" and make an Examination of Conscience. (Chapter 2)
- Pray for your confessor.

During Confession
- Priest welcomes you. Make the Sign of the Cross.
- Say "**Bless me Father, for I have sinned, this is my First Confession,**" or "**Bless me Father, for I have sinned, my last Confession was _____ (days, weeks, months) ago.**"
- Tell the priest your sins below:

✔	The Lord says, "You Shall Love the Lord Your God with your whole heart."	# Of Times?
	I did not obey God right away.	
	I doubted God's love for me.	
	I did not use all the graces God gave me to become closer to Him.	
	I did not pray my daily prayers (morning, evening, meals).	
	I put other things before God (friends, toys, games, and money).	
	I did not try to do my best for Jesus, even when I had to do things I didn't want to.	
	I spent money unwisely.	
	I placed my faith things other than God (good luck charms, etc.)	
	I said God's name in anger or frustration and / or spoke disrespectfully of God or Our Lady.	
	I used bad words (swear words).	
	I did not show reverence toward sacred persons, places, and things (e.g., the Pope, Bishop, priests, nuns, brothers, crucifixes, sacramentals, etc.).	
	I missed Mass on purpose on a Sunday or Holy Day of Obligation.	
	I was late for Mass or my behavior played a factor in our being late for Mass.	
	I did not abstain or fast according to Church teaching (one hour before receiving Jesus in Eucharist, no meat on Friday during Lent, etc.).	
	I laughed or distracted others in church.	
✔	The Lord Says, "You shall love your neighbor as yourself,"	
	I did not give my parent, guardian, or teacher right-away obedience.	
	I was disrespectful to my parent, guardian, or teacher.	

"The confession of evil works is the first beginning of good works."—St. Augustine

I did not do my chores without grumbling or needing to be nagged.	
I spoke uncharitably to my parent, guardian, teacher, friend, sibling, etc.	
I lied.	
I took something that did not belong to me.	
I teased someone.	
I hurt someone.	
I did not treat my body, a temple of the Holy Spirit, with respect (ate too much, dressed immodestly, avoided exercise, etc.).	
I did not respect other's personal space.	
I said unkind words to or about someone else.	
I became envious of something someone else has or has achieved.	
I became angry or envious and did not handle my feelings in a positive way.	
I was prideful or boastful.	
I could have helped somebody and chose not to.	
I could have shared and chose not to.	
I could have been charitable and chose not to.	

- Say, "**I am sorry for these and all of my sins.**"
- Listen to the priest and pray an **Act of Contrition**:

   Act of Contrition - My God, I am sorry for my sins with all my heart. In choosing to do wrong and failing to do good, I have sinned against You whom I should love above all things. I firmly intend, with Your help, to do penance, to sin no more, and to avoid whatever leads me to sin. Our Savior Jesus Christ suffered and died for us. In His Name, my God, have mercy. Amen.

   Or

   Act of Contrition: O my God, I am heartily sorry for having offended You and I detest all my sins, because I dread the loss of heaven and the pains of hell. But most of all because I have offended You, my God, who are all good and deserving of all my love. I firmly resolve with the help of Your grace, to confess my sins, to do penance and to amend my life. Amen.

- Priest will say words of absolution (forgiveness). Make the Sign of the Cross.
- If he closes by saying, "Give thanks to the Lord for He is good," answer, **"For His mercy endures forever."**
- Perform your penance.
- Thank God.

"The confession of evil works is the first beginning of good works."—St. Augustine

Today's Date: _____

Before Confession:

- Pray, "Come Holy Spirit" and make an Examination of Conscience. (Chapter 2)
- Pray for your confessor.

During Confession

- Priest welcomes you. Make the Sign of the Cross.
- Say "**Bless me Father, for I have sinned, this is my First Confession,**" or "**Bless me Father, for I have sinned, my last Confession was** _____ (**days, weeks, months**) **ago.**"
- Tell the priest your sins below:

✔	The Lord says, "You Shall Love the Lord Your God with your whole heart."	# Of Times?
	I did not obey God right away.	
	I doubted God's love for me.	
	I did not use all the graces God gave me to become closer to Him.	
	I did not pray my daily prayers (morning, evening, meals).	
	I put other things before God (friends, toys, games, and money).	
	I did not try to do my best for Jesus, even when I had to do things I didn't want to.	
	I spent money unwisely.	
	I placed my faith things other than God (good luck charms, etc.)	
	I said God's name in anger or frustration and / or spoke disrespectfully of God or Our Lady.	
	I used bad words (swear words).	
	I did not show reverence toward sacred persons, places, and things (e.g., the Pope, Bishop, priests, nuns, brothers, crucifixes, sacramentals, etc.).	
	I missed Mass on purpose on a Sunday or Holy Day of Obligation.	
	I was late for Mass or my behavior played a factor in our being late for Mass.	
	I did not abstain or fast according to Church teaching (one hour before receiving Jesus in Eucharist, no meat on Friday during Lent, etc.).	
	I laughed or distracted others in church.	
✔	The Lord Says, "You shall love your neighbor as yourself,"	
	I did not give my parent, guardian, or teacher right-away obedience.	
	I was disrespectful to my parent, guardian, or teacher.	

"The confession of evil works is the first beginning of good works."—St. Augustine

I did not do my chores without grumbling or needing to be nagged.	
I spoke uncharitably to my parent, guardian, teacher, friend, sibling, etc.	
I lied.	
I took something that did not belong to me.	
I teased someone.	
I hurt someone.	
I did not treat my body, a temple of the Holy Spirit, with respect (ate too much, dressed immodestly, avoided exercise, etc.).	
I did not respect other's personal space.	
I said unkind words to or about someone else.	
I became envious of something someone else has or has achieved.	
I became angry or envious and did not handle my feelings in a positive way.	
I was prideful or boastful.	
I could have helped somebody and chose not to.	
I could have shared and chose not to.	
I could have been charitable and chose not to.	

- Say, "**I am sorry for these and all of my sins.**"
- Listen to the priest and pray an **Act of Contrition**:
  Act of Contrition - My God, I am sorry for my sins with all my heart. In choosing to do wrong and failing to do good, I have sinned against You whom I should love above all things. I firmly intend, with Your help, to do penance, to sin no more, and to avoid whatever leads me to sin. Our Savior Jesus Christ suffered and died for us. In His Name, my God, have mercy. Amen.
  Or
  Act of Contrition: O my God, I am heartily sorry for having offended You and I detest all my sins, because I dread the loss of heaven and the pains of hell. But most of all because I have offended You, my God, who are all good and deserving of all my love. I firmly resolve with the help of Your grace, to confess my sins, to do penance and to amend my life. Amen.

- Priest will say words of absolution (forgiveness). Make the Sign of the Cross.
- If he closes by saying, "Give thanks to the Lord for He is good," answer, **"For His mercy endures forever."**
- Perform your penance.
- Thank God.

"The confession of evil works is the first beginning of good works."—St. Augustine

Today's Date: _____

Before Confession:

- Pray, "Come Holy Spirit" and make an Examination of Conscience. (Chapter 2)
- Pray for your confessor.

During Confession

- Priest welcomes you. Make the Sign of the Cross.
- Say **"Bless me Father, for I have sinned, this is my First Confession,"** or **"Bless me Father, for I have sinned, my last Confession was _____ (days, weeks, months) ago."**
- Tell the priest your sins below:

✔	The Lord says, "You Shall Love the Lord Your God with your whole heart."	# Of Times?
	I did not obey God right away.	
	I doubted God's love for me.	
	I did not use all the graces God gave me to become closer to Him.	
	I did not pray my daily prayers (morning, evening, meals).	
	I put other things before God (friends, toys, games, and money).	
	I did not try to do my best for Jesus, even when I had to do things I didn't want to.	
	I spent money unwisely.	
	I placed my faith things other than God (good luck charms, etc.)	
	I said God's name in anger or frustration and / or spoke disrespectfully of God or Our Lady.	
	I used bad words (swear words).	
	I did not show reverence toward sacred persons, places, and things (e.g., the Pope, Bishop, priests, nuns, brothers, crucifixes, sacramentals, etc.).	
	I missed Mass on purpose on a Sunday or Holy Day of Obligation.	
	I was late for Mass or my behavior played a factor in our being late for Mass.	
	I did not abstain or fast according to Church teaching (one hour before receiving Jesus in Eucharist, no meat on Friday during Lent, etc.).	
	I laughed or distracted others in church.	
✔	The Lord Says, "You shall love your neighbor as yourself."	
	I did not give my parent, guardian, or teacher right-away obedience.	
	I was disrespectful to my parent, guardian, or teacher.	

"The confession of evil works is the first beginning of good works."—St. Augustine

I did not do my chores without grumbling or needing to be nagged.	
I spoke uncharitably to my parent, guardian, teacher, friend, sibling, etc.	
I lied.	
I took something that did not belong to me.	
I teased someone.	
I hurt someone.	
I did not treat my body, a temple of the Holy Spirit, with respect (ate too much, dressed immodestly, avoided exercise, etc.).	
I did not respect other's personal space.	
I said unkind words to or about someone else.	
I became envious of something someone else has or has achieved.	
I became angry or envious and did not handle my feelings in a positive way.	
I was prideful or boastful.	
I could have helped somebody and chose not to.	
I could have shared and chose not to.	
I could have been charitable and chose not to.	

- Say, "**I am sorry for these and all of my sins.**"
- Listen to the priest and pray an **Act of Contrition**:
  Act of Contrition - My God, I am sorry for my sins with all my heart. In choosing to do wrong and failing to do good, I have sinned against You whom I should love above all things. I firmly intend, with Your help, to do penance, to sin no more, and to avoid whatever leads me to sin. Our Savior Jesus Christ suffered and died for us. In His Name, my God, have mercy. Amen.
  Or
  Act of Contrition: O my God, I am heartily sorry for having offended You and I detest all my sins, because I dread the loss of heaven and the pains of hell. But most of all because I have offended You, my God, who are all good and deserving of all my love. I firmly resolve with the help of Your grace, to confess my sins, to do penance and to amend my life. Amen.

- Priest will say words of absolution (forgiveness). Make the Sign of the Cross.
- If he closes by saying, "Give thanks to the Lord for He is good," answer, **"For His mercy endures forever."**
- Perform your penance.
- Thank God.

"The confession of evil works is the first beginning of good works."—St. Augustine

Today's Date: _____

Before Confession:
- Pray, "Come Holy Spirit" and make an Examination of Conscience. (Chapter 2)
- Pray for your confessor.

During Confession
- Priest welcomes you. Make the Sign of the Cross.
- Say **"Bless me Father, for I have sinned, this is my First Confession,"** or **"Bless me Father, for I have sinned, my last Confession was _____ (days, weeks, months) ago."**
- Tell the priest your sins below:

✔ The Lord says, "You Shall Love the Lord Your God with your whole heart."	# Of Times?
I did not obey God right away.	
I doubted God's love for me.	
I did not use all the graces God gave me to become closer to Him.	
I did not pray my daily prayers (morning, evening, meals).	
I put other things before God (friends, toys, games, and money).	
I did not try to do my best for Jesus, even when I had to do things I didn't want to.	
I spent money unwisely.	
I placed my faith things other than God (good luck charms, etc.)	
I said God's name in anger or frustration and / or spoke disrespectfully of God or Our Lady.	
I used bad words (swear words).	
I did not show reverence toward sacred persons, places, and things (e.g., the Pope, Bishop, priests, nuns, brothers, crucifixes, sacramentals, etc.).	
I missed Mass on purpose on a Sunday or Holy Day of Obligation.	
I was late for Mass or my behavior played a factor in our being late for Mass.	
I did not abstain or fast according to Church teaching (one hour before receiving Jesus in Eucharist, no meat on Friday during Lent, etc.).	
I laughed or distracted others in church.	
✔ The Lord Says, "You shall love your neighbor as yourself,"	
I did not give my parent, guardian, or teacher right-away obedience.	
I was disrespectful to my parent, guardian, or teacher.	

"The confession of evil works is the first beginning of good works."—*St. Augustine*

I did not do my chores without grumbling or needing to be nagged.	
I spoke uncharitably to my parent, guardian, teacher, friend, sibling, etc.	
I lied.	
I took something that did not belong to me.	
I teased someone.	
I hurt someone.	
I did not treat my body, a temple of the Holy Spirit, with respect (ate too much, dressed immodestly, avoided exercise, etc.).	
I did not respect other's personal space.	
I said unkind words to or about someone else.	
I became envious of something someone else has or has achieved.	
I became angry or envious and did not handle my feelings in a positive way.	
I was prideful or boastful.	
I could have helped somebody and chose not to.	
I could have shared and chose not to.	
I could have been charitable and chose not to.	

- Say, "**I am sorry for these and all of my sins.**"
- Listen to the priest and pray an **Act of Contrition**:

  Act of Contrition - My God, I am sorry for my sins with all my heart. In choosing to do wrong and failing to do good, I have sinned against You whom I should love above all things. I firmly intend, with Your help, to do penance, to sin no more, and to avoid whatever leads me to sin. Our Savior Jesus Christ suffered and died for us. In His Name, my God, have mercy. Amen.

  Or

  Act of Contrition: O my God, I am heartily sorry for having offended You and I detest all my sins, because I dread the loss of heaven and the pains of hell. But most of all because I have offended You, my God, who are all good and deserving of all my love. I firmly resolve with the help of Your grace, to confess my sins, to do penance and to amend my life. Amen.

- Priest will say words of absolution (forgiveness). Make the Sign of the Cross.
- If he closes by saying, "Give thanks to the Lord for He is good," answer, "**For His mercy endures forever.**"
- Perform your penance.
- Thank God.

"The confession of evil works is the first beginning of good works."—St. Augustine

Today's Date: _____

Before Confession:
- Pray, "Come Holy Spirit" and make an Examination of Conscience. (Chapter 2)
- Pray for your confessor.

During Confession
- Priest welcomes you. Make the Sign of the Cross.
- Say **"Bless me Father, for I have sinned, this is my First Confession,"** or **"Bless me Father, for I have sinned, my last Confession was _____ (days, weeks, months) ago."**
- Tell the priest your sins below:

✔ The Lord says, "You Shall Love the Lord Your God with your whole heart."	# Of Times?
I did not obey God right away.	
I doubted God's love for me.	
I did not use all the graces God gave me to become closer to Him.	
I did not pray my daily prayers (morning, evening, meals).	
I put other things before God (friends, toys, games, and money).	
I did not try to do my best for Jesus, even when I had to do things I didn't want to.	
I spent money unwisely.	
I placed my faith things other than God (good luck charms, etc.)	
I said God's name in anger or frustration and / or spoke disrespectfully of God or Our Lady.	
I used bad words (swear words).	
I did not show reverence toward sacred persons, places, and things (e.g., the Pope, Bishop, priests, nuns, brothers, crucifixes, sacramentals, etc.).	
I missed Mass on purpose on a Sunday or Holy Day of Obligation.	
I was late for Mass or my behavior played a factor in our being late for Mass.	
I did not abstain or fast according to Church teaching (one hour before receiving Jesus in Eucharist, no meat on Friday during Lent, etc.).	
I laughed or distracted others in church.	
✔ The Lord Says, "You shall love your neighbor as yourself,"	
I did not give my parent, guardian, or teacher right-away obedience.	
I was disrespectful to my parent, guardian, or teacher.	

"The confession of evil works is the first beginning of good works."—St. Augustine

I did not do my chores without grumbling or needing to be nagged.	
I spoke uncharitably to my parent, guardian, teacher, friend, sibling, etc.	
I lied.	
I took something that did not belong to me.	
I teased someone.	
I hurt someone.	
I did not treat my body, a temple of the Holy Spirit, with respect (ate too much, dressed immodestly, avoided exercise, etc.).	
I did not respect other's personal space.	
I said unkind words to or about someone else.	
I became envious of something someone else has or has achieved.	
I became angry or envious and did not handle my feelings in a positive way.	
I was prideful or boastful.	
I could have helped somebody and chose not to.	
I could have shared and chose not to.	
I could have been charitable and chose not to.	

- Say, "**I am sorry for these and all of my sins.**"
- Listen to the priest and pray an **Act of Contrition**:
  Act of Contrition - My God, I am sorry for my sins with all my heart. In choosing to do wrong and failing to do good, I have sinned against You whom I should love above all things. I firmly intend, with Your help, to do penance, to sin no more, and to avoid whatever leads me to sin. Our Savior Jesus Christ suffered and died for us. In His Name, my God, have mercy. Amen.
  Or
  Act of Contrition: O my God, I am heartily sorry for having offended You and I detest all my sins, because I dread the loss of heaven and the pains of hell. But most of all because I have offended You, my God, who are all good and deserving of all my love. I firmly resolve with the help of Your grace, to confess my sins, to do penance and to amend my life. Amen.

- Priest will say words of absolution (forgiveness). Make the Sign of the Cross.
- If he closes by saying, "Give thanks to the Lord for He is good," answer, **"For His mercy endures forever."**
- Perform your penance.
- Thank God.

"The confession of evil works is the first beginning of good works."—St. Augustine

Today's Date: _____

Before Confession:

- Pray, "Come Holy Spirit" and make an Examination of Conscience. (Chapter 2)
- Pray for your confessor.

During Confession

- Priest welcomes you. Make the Sign of the Cross.
- Say "**Bless me Father, for I have sinned, this is my First Confession,**" or "**Bless me Father, for I have sinned, my last Confession was** _____ (**days, weeks, months**) **ago.**"
- Tell the priest your sins below:

✔	The Lord says, "You Shall Love the Lord Your God with your whole heart."	# Of Times?
	I did not obey God right away.	
	I doubted God's love for me.	
	I did not use all the graces God gave me to become closer to Him.	
	I did not pray my daily prayers (morning, evening, meals).	
	I put other things before God (friends, toys, games, and money).	
	I did not try to do my best for Jesus, even when I had to do things I didn't want to.	
	I spent money unwisely.	
	I placed my faith things other than God (good luck charms, etc.)	
	I said God's name in anger or frustration and / or spoke disrespectfully of God or Our Lady.	
	I used bad words (swear words).	
	I did not show reverence toward sacred persons, places, and things (e.g., the Pope, Bishop, priests, nuns, brothers, crucifixes, sacramentals, etc.).	
	I missed Mass on purpose on a Sunday or Holy Day of Obligation.	
	I was late for Mass or my behavior played a factor in our being late for Mass.	
	I did not abstain or fast according to Church teaching (one hour before receiving Jesus in Eucharist, no meat on Friday during Lent, etc.).	
	I laughed or distracted others in church.	
✔	The Lord Says, "You shall love your neighbor as yourself,"	
	I did not give my parent, guardian, or teacher right-away obedience.	
	I was disrespectful to my parent, guardian, or teacher.	

"The confession of evil works is the first beginning of good works."—St. Augustine

I did not do my chores without grumbling or needing to be nagged.	
I spoke uncharitably to my parent, guardian, teacher, friend, sibling, etc.	
I lied.	
I took something that did not belong to me.	
I teased someone.	
I hurt someone.	
I did not treat my body, a temple of the Holy Spirit, with respect (ate too much, dressed immodestly, avoided exercise, etc.).	
I did not respect other's personal space.	
I said unkind words to or about someone else.	
I became envious of something someone else has or has achieved.	
I became angry or envious and did not handle my feelings in a positive way.	
I was prideful or boastful.	
I could have helped somebody and chose not to.	
I could have shared and chose not to.	
I could have been charitable and chose not to.	

- Say, "**I am sorry for these and all of my sins.**"
- Listen to the priest and pray an **Act of Contrition**:
  Act of Contrition - My God, I am sorry for my sins with all my heart. In choosing to do wrong and failing to do good, I have sinned against You whom I should love above all things. I firmly intend, with Your help, to do penance, to sin no more, and to avoid whatever leads me to sin. Our Savior Jesus Christ suffered and died for us. In His Name, my God, have mercy. Amen.
  Or
  Act of Contrition: O my God, I am heartily sorry for having offended You and I detest all my sins, because I dread the loss of heaven and the pains of hell. But most of all because I have offended You, my God, who are all good and deserving of all my love. I firmly resolve with the help of Your grace, to confess my sins, to do penance and to amend my life. Amen.

- Priest will say words of absolution (forgiveness). Make the Sign of the Cross.
- If he closes by saying, "Give thanks to the Lord for He is good," answer, "**For His mercy endures forever.**"
- Perform your penance.
- Thank God.

"The confession of evil works is the first beginning of good works."—St. Augustine

Today's Date: _____

Before Confession:
- Pray, "Come Holy Spirit" and make an Examination of Conscience. (Chapter 2)
- Pray for your confessor.

During Confession
- Priest welcomes you. Make the Sign of the Cross.
- Say "**Bless me Father, for I have sinned, this is my First Confession,**" or "**Bless me Father, for I have sinned, my last Confession was _____ (days, weeks, months) ago.**"
- Tell the priest your sins below:

✔	The Lord says, "You Shall Love the Lord Your God with your whole heart."	# Of Times?
	I did not obey God right away.	
	I doubted God's love for me.	
	I did not use all the graces God gave me to become closer to Him.	
	I did not pray my daily prayers (morning, evening, meals).	
	I put other things before God (friends, toys, games, and money).	
	I did not try to do my best for Jesus, even when I had to do things I didn't want to.	
	I spent money unwisely.	
	I placed my faith things other than God (good luck charms, etc.)	
	I said God's name in anger or frustration and / or spoke disrespectfully of God or Our Lady.	
	I used bad words (swear words).	
	I did not show reverence toward sacred persons, places, and things (e.g., the Pope, Bishop, priests, nuns, brothers, crucifixes, sacramentals, etc.).	
	I missed Mass on purpose on a Sunday or Holy Day of Obligation.	
	I was late for Mass or my behavior played a factor in our being late for Mass.	
	I did not abstain or fast according to Church teaching (one hour before receiving Jesus in Eucharist, no meat on Friday during Lent, etc.).	
	I laughed or distracted others in church.	
✔	The Lord Says, "You shall love your neighbor as yourself,"	
	I did not give my parent, guardian, or teacher right-away obedience.	
	I was disrespectful to my parent, guardian, or teacher.	

"The confession of evil works is the first beginning of good works."—St. Augustine

I did not do my chores without grumbling or needing to be nagged.	
I spoke uncharitably to my parent, guardian, teacher, friend, sibling, etc.	
I lied.	
I took something that did not belong to me.	
I teased someone.	
I hurt someone.	
I did not treat my body, a temple of the Holy Spirit, with respect (ate too much, dressed immodestly, avoided exercise, etc.).	
I did not respect other's personal space.	
I said unkind words to or about someone else.	
I became envious of something someone else has or has achieved.	
I became angry or envious and did not handle my feelings in a positive way.	
I was prideful or boastful.	
I could have helped somebody and chose not to.	
I could have shared and chose not to.	
I could have been charitable and chose not to.	

- Say, "**I am sorry for these and all of my sins.**"
- Listen to the priest and pray an **Act of Contrition**:
  Act of Contrition - My God, I am sorry for my sins with all my heart. In choosing to do wrong and failing to do good, I have sinned against You whom I should love above all things. I firmly intend, with Your help, to do penance, to sin no more, and to avoid whatever leads me to sin. Our Savior Jesus Christ suffered and died for us. In His Name, my God, have mercy. Amen.
  Or
  Act of Contrition: O my God, I am heartily sorry for having offended You and I detest all my sins, because I dread the loss of heaven and the pains of hell. But most of all because I have offended You, my God, who are all good and deserving of all my love. I firmly resolve with the help of Your grace, to confess my sins, to do penance and to amend my life. Amen.

- Priest will say words of absolution (forgiveness). Make the Sign of the Cross.
- If he closes by saying, "Give thanks to the Lord for He is good," answer, **"For His mercy endures forever."**
- Perform your penance.
- Thank God.

"The confession of evil works is the first beginning of good works."—*St. Augustine*

Today's Date: _____

Before Confession:

- Pray, "Come Holy Spirit" and make an Examination of Conscience. (Chapter 2)
- Pray for your confessor.

During Confession

- Priest welcomes you. Make the Sign of the Cross.
- Say "**Bless me Father, for I have sinned, this is my First Confession,**" or "**Bless me Father, for I have sinned, my last Confession was _____ (days, weeks, months) ago.**"
- Tell the priest your sins below:

✔	The Lord says, "You Shall Love the Lord Your God with your whole heart."	# Of Times?
	I did not obey God right away.	
	I doubted God's love for me.	
	I did not use all the graces God gave me to become closer to Him.	
	I did not pray my daily prayers (morning, evening, meals).	
	I put other things before God (friends, toys, games, and money).	
	I did not try to do my best for Jesus, even when I had to do things I didn't want to.	
	I spent money unwisely.	
	I placed my faith things other than God (good luck charms, etc.)	
	I said God's name in anger or frustration and / or spoke disrespectfully of God or Our Lady.	
	I used bad words (swear words).	
	I did not show reverence toward sacred persons, places, and things (e.g., the Pope, Bishop, priests, nuns, brothers, crucifixes, sacramentals, etc.).	
	I missed Mass on purpose on a Sunday or Holy Day of Obligation.	
	I was late for Mass or my behavior played a factor in our being late for Mass.	
	I did not abstain or fast according to Church teaching (one hour before receiving Jesus in Eucharist, no meat on Friday during Lent, etc.).	
	I laughed or distracted others in church.	
✔	The Lord Says, "You shall love your neighbor as yourself,"	
	I did not give my parent, guardian, or teacher right-away obedience.	
	I was disrespectful to my parent, guardian, or teacher.	

"The confession of evil works is the first beginning of good works."—St. Augustine

I did not do my chores without grumbling or needing to be nagged.	
I spoke uncharitably to my parent, guardian, teacher, friend, sibling, etc.	
I lied.	
I took something that did not belong to me.	
I teased someone.	
I hurt someone.	
I did not treat my body, a temple of the Holy Spirit, with respect (ate too much, dressed immodestly, avoided exercise, etc.).	
I did not respect other's personal space.	
I said unkind words to or about someone else.	
I became envious of something someone else has or has achieved.	
I became angry or envious and did not handle my feelings in a positive way.	
I was prideful or boastful.	
I could have helped somebody and chose not to.	
I could have shared and chose not to.	
I could have been charitable and chose not to.	

- Say, "**I am sorry for these and all of my sins.**"
- Listen to the priest and pray an **Act of Contrition**:

  Act of Contrition - My God, I am sorry for my sins with all my heart. In choosing to do wrong and failing to do good, I have sinned against You whom I should love above all things. I firmly intend, with Your help, to do penance, to sin no more, and to avoid whatever leads me to sin. Our Savior Jesus Christ suffered and died for us. In His Name, my God, have mercy. Amen.

  Or

  Act of Contrition: O my God, I am heartily sorry for having offended You and I detest all my sins, because I dread the loss of heaven and the pains of hell. But most of all because I have offended You, my God, who are all good and deserving of all my love. I firmly resolve with the help of Your grace, to confess my sins, to do penance and to amend my life. Amen.

- Priest will say words of absolution (forgiveness). Make the Sign of the Cross.
- If he closes by saying, "Give thanks to the Lord for He is good," answer, **"For His mercy endures forever."**
- Perform your penance.
- Thank God.

"The confession of evil works is the first beginning of good works."—St. Augustine

Today's Date: _____

Before Confession:

- Pray, "Come Holy Spirit" and make an Examination of Conscience. (Chapter 2)
- Pray for your confessor.

During Confession

- Priest welcomes you. Make the Sign of the Cross.
- Say **"Bless me Father, for I have sinned, this is my First Confession,"** or **"Bless me Father, for I have sinned, my last Confession was _____ (days, weeks, months) ago."**
- Tell the priest your sins below:

✔	The Lord says, "You Shall Love the Lord Your God with your whole heart."	# Of Times?
	I did not obey God right away.	
	I doubted God's love for me.	
	I did not use all the graces God gave me to become closer to Him.	
	I did not pray my daily prayers (morning, evening, meals).	
	I put other things before God (friends, toys, games, and money).	
	I did not try to do my best for Jesus, even when I had to do things I didn't want to.	
	I spent money unwisely.	
	I placed my faith things other than God (good luck charms, etc.)	
	I said God's name in anger or frustration and / or spoke disrespectfully of God or Our Lady.	
	I used bad words (swear words).	
	I did not show reverence toward sacred persons, places, and things (e.g., the Pope, Bishop, priests, nuns, brothers, crucifixes, sacramentals, etc.).	
	I missed Mass on purpose on a Sunday or Holy Day of Obligation.	
	I was late for Mass or my behavior played a factor in our being late for Mass.	
	I did not abstain or fast according to Church teaching (one hour before receiving Jesus in Eucharist, no meat on Friday during Lent, etc.).	
	I laughed or distracted others in church.	
✔	The Lord Says, "You shall love your neighbor as yourself,"	
	I did not give my parent, guardian, or teacher right-away obedience.	
	I was disrespectful to my parent, guardian, or teacher.	

"The confession of evil works is the first beginning of good works."—St. Augustine

I did not do my chores without grumbling or needing to be nagged.	
I spoke uncharitably to my parent, guardian, teacher, friend, sibling, etc.	
I lied.	
I took something that did not belong to me.	
I teased someone.	
I hurt someone.	
I did not treat my body, a temple of the Holy Spirit, with respect (ate too much, dressed immodestly, avoided exercise, etc.).	
I did not respect other's personal space.	
I said unkind words to or about someone else.	
I became envious of something someone else has or has achieved.	
I became angry or envious and did not handle my feelings in a positive way.	
I was prideful or boastful.	
I could have helped somebody and chose not to.	
I could have shared and chose not to.	
I could have been charitable and chose not to.	

- Say, "**I am sorry for these and all of my sins.**"
- Listen to the priest and pray an **Act of Contrition**:
  Act of Contrition - My God, I am sorry for my sins with all my heart. In choosing to do wrong and failing to do good, I have sinned against You whom I should love above all things. I firmly intend, with Your help, to do penance, to sin no more, and to avoid whatever leads me to sin. Our Savior Jesus Christ suffered and died for us. In His Name, my God, have mercy. Amen.
  Or
  Act of Contrition: O my God, I am heartily sorry for having offended You and I detest all my sins, because I dread the loss of heaven and the pains of hell. But most of all because I have offended You, my God, who are all good and deserving of all my love. I firmly resolve with the help of Your grace, to confess my sins, to do penance and to amend my life. Amen.

- Priest will say words of absolution (forgiveness). Make the Sign of the Cross.
- If he closes by saying, "Give thanks to the Lord for He is good," answer, **"For His mercy endures forever."**
- Perform your penance.
- Thank God.

"The confession of evil works is the first beginning of good works."—St. Augustine

Today's Date: _____

Before Confession:
- Pray, "Come Holy Spirit" and make an Examination of Conscience. (Chapter 2)
- Pray for your confessor.

During Confession
- Priest welcomes you. Make the Sign of the Cross.
- Say "**Bless me Father, for I have sinned, this is my First Confession,**" or "**Bless me Father, for I have sinned, my last Confession was** _____ **(days, weeks, months) ago.**"
- Tell the priest your sins below:

✔ The Lord says, "You Shall Love the Lord Your God with your whole heart."	# Of Times?
I did not obey God right away.	
I doubted God's love for me.	
I did not use all the graces God gave me to become closer to Him.	
I did not pray my daily prayers (morning, evening, meals).	
I put other things before God (friends, toys, games, and money).	
I did not try to do my best for Jesus, even when I had to do things I didn't want to.	
I spent money unwisely.	
I placed my faith things other than God (good luck charms, etc.)	
I said God's name in anger or frustration and / or spoke disrespectfully of God or Our Lady.	
I used bad words (swear words).	
I did not show reverence toward sacred persons, places, and things (e.g., the Pope, Bishop, priests, nuns, brothers, crucifixes, sacramentals, etc.).	
I missed Mass on purpose on a Sunday or Holy Day of Obligation.	
I was late for Mass or my behavior played a factor in our being late for Mass.	
I did not abstain or fast according to Church teaching (one hour before receiving Jesus in Eucharist, no meat on Friday during Lent, etc.).	
I laughed or distracted others in church.	
✔ The Lord Says, "You shall love your neighbor as yourself,"	
I did not give my parent, guardian, or teacher right-away obedience.	
I was disrespectful to my parent, guardian, or teacher.	

"The confession of evil works is the first beginning of good works."—St. Augustine

I did not do my chores without grumbling or needing to be nagged.	
I spoke uncharitably to my parent, guardian, teacher, friend, sibling, etc.	
I lied.	
I took something that did not belong to me.	
I teased someone.	
I hurt someone.	
I did not treat my body, a temple of the Holy Spirit, with respect (ate too much, dressed immodestly, avoided exercise, etc.).	
I did not respect other's personal space.	
I said unkind words to or about someone else.	
I became envious of something someone else has or has achieved.	
I became angry or envious and did not handle my feelings in a positive way.	
I was prideful or boastful.	
I could have helped somebody and chose not to.	
I could have shared and chose not to.	
I could have been charitable and chose not to.	

- Say, "**I am sorry for these and all of my sins.**"
- Listen to the priest and pray an **Act of Contrition**:
  Act of Contrition - My God, I am sorry for my sins with all my heart. In choosing to do wrong and failing to do good, I have sinned against You whom I should love above all things. I firmly intend, with Your help, to do penance, to sin no more, and to avoid whatever leads me to sin. Our Savior Jesus Christ suffered and died for us. In His Name, my God, have mercy. Amen.
  Or
  Act of Contrition: O my God, I am heartily sorry for having offended You and I detest all my sins, because I dread the loss of heaven and the pains of hell. But most of all because I have offended You, my God, who are all good and deserving of all my love. I firmly resolve with the help of Your grace, to confess my sins, to do penance and to amend my life. Amen.

- Priest will say words of absolution (forgiveness). Make the Sign of the Cross.
- If he closes by saying, "Give thanks to the Lord for He is good," answer, **"For His mercy endures forever."**
- Perform your penance.
- Thank God.

"The confession of evil works is the first beginning of good works."—*St. Augustine*

Today's Date: _____

Before Confession:

- Pray, "Come Holy Spirit" and make an Examination of Conscience. (Chapter 2)
- Pray for your confessor.

During Confession

- Priest welcomes you. Make the Sign of the Cross.
- Say "**Bless me Father, for I have sinned, this is my First Confession,**" or "**Bless me Father, for I have sinned, my last Confession was** _____ **(days, weeks, months) ago.**"
- Tell the priest your sins below:

✔	The Lord says, "You Shall Love the Lord Your God with your whole heart."	# Of Times?
	I did not obey God right away.	
	I doubted God's love for me.	
	I did not use all the graces God gave me to become closer to Him.	
	I did not pray my daily prayers (morning, evening, meals).	
	I put other things before God (friends, toys, games, and money).	
	I did not try to do my best for Jesus, even when I had to do things I didn't want to.	
	I spent money unwisely.	
	I placed my faith things other than God (good luck charms, etc.)	
	I said God's name in anger or frustration and / or spoke disrespectfully of God or Our Lady.	
	I used bad words (swear words).	
	I did not show reverence toward sacred persons, places, and things (e.g., the Pope, Bishop, priests, nuns, brothers, crucifixes, sacramentals, etc.).	
	I missed Mass on purpose on a Sunday or Holy Day of Obligation.	
	I was late for Mass or my behavior played a factor in our being late for Mass.	
	I did not abstain or fast according to Church teaching (one hour before receiving Jesus in Eucharist, no meat on Friday during Lent, etc.).	
	I laughed or distracted others in church.	
✔	The Lord Says, "You shall love your neighbor as yourself,"	
	I did not give my parent, guardian, or teacher right-away obedience.	
	I was disrespectful to my parent, guardian, or teacher.	

"The confession of evil works is the first beginning of good works."—St. Augustine

I did not do my chores without grumbling or needing to be nagged.	
I spoke uncharitably to my parent, guardian, teacher, friend, sibling, etc.	
I lied.	
I took something that did not belong to me.	
I teased someone.	
I hurt someone.	
I did not treat my body, a temple of the Holy Spirit, with respect (ate too much, dressed immodestly, avoided exercise, etc.).	
I did not respect other's personal space.	
I said unkind words to or about someone else.	
I became envious of something someone else has or has achieved.	
I became angry or envious and did not handle my feelings in a positive way.	
I was prideful or boastful.	
I could have helped somebody and chose not to.	
I could have shared and chose not to.	
I could have been charitable and chose not to.	

- Say, "**I am sorry for these and all of my sins.**"
- Listen to the priest and pray an **Act of Contrition**:
  Act of Contrition - My God, I am sorry for my sins with all my heart. In choosing to do wrong and failing to do good, I have sinned against You whom I should love above all things. I firmly intend, with Your help, to do penance, to sin no more, and to avoid whatever leads me to sin. Our Savior Jesus Christ suffered and died for us. In His Name, my God, have mercy. Amen.
  Or
  Act of Contrition: O my God, I am heartily sorry for having offended You and I detest all my sins, because I dread the loss of heaven and the pains of hell. But most of all because I have offended You, my God, who are all good and deserving of all my love. I firmly resolve with the help of Your grace, to confess my sins, to do penance and to amend my life. Amen.

- Priest will say words of absolution (forgiveness). Make the Sign of the Cross.
- If he closes by saying, "Give thanks to the Lord for He is good," answer, **"For His mercy endures forever."**
- Perform your penance.
- Thank God.

"The confession of evil works is the first beginning of good works."—St. Augustine

Today's Date: _____

Before Confession:
- Pray, "Come Holy Spirit" and make an Examination of Conscience. (Chapter 2)
- Pray for your confessor.

During Confession
- Priest welcomes you. Make the Sign of the Cross.
- Say **"Bless me Father, for I have sinned, this is my First Confession,"** or **"Bless me Father, for I have sinned, my last Confession was _____ (days, weeks, months) ago."**
- Tell the priest your sins below:

✔ The Lord says, "You Shall Love the Lord Your God with your whole heart."	# Of Times?
I did not obey God right away.	
I doubted God's love for me.	
I did not use all the graces God gave me to become closer to Him.	
I did not pray my daily prayers (morning, evening, meals).	
I put other things before God (friends, toys, games, and money).	
I did not try to do my best for Jesus, even when I had to do things I didn't want to.	
I spent money unwisely.	
I placed my faith things other than God (good luck charms, etc.)	
I said God's name in anger or frustration and / or spoke disrespectfully of God or Our Lady.	
I used bad words (swear words).	
I did not show reverence toward sacred persons, places, and things (e.g., the Pope, Bishop, priests, nuns, brothers, crucifixes, sacramentals, etc.).	
I missed Mass on purpose on a Sunday or Holy Day of Obligation.	
I was late for Mass or my behavior played a factor in our being late for Mass.	
I did not abstain or fast according to Church teaching (one hour before receiving Jesus in Eucharist, no meat on Friday during Lent, etc.).	
I laughed or distracted others in church.	
✔ The Lord Says, "You shall love your neighbor as yourself,"	
I did not give my parent, guardian, or teacher right-away obedience.	
I was disrespectful to my parent, guardian, or teacher.	

"The confession of evil works is the first beginning of good works."—*St. Augustine*

I did not do my chores without grumbling or needing to be nagged.	
I spoke uncharitably to my parent, guardian, teacher, friend, sibling, etc.	
I lied.	
I took something that did not belong to me.	
I teased someone.	
I hurt someone.	
I did not treat my body, a temple of the Holy Spirit, with respect (ate too much, dressed immodestly, avoided exercise, etc.).	
I did not respect other's personal space.	
I said unkind words to or about someone else.	
I became envious of something someone else has or has achieved.	
I became angry or envious and did not handle my feelings in a positive way.	
I was prideful or boastful.	
I could have helped somebody and chose not to.	
I could have shared and chose not to.	
I could have been charitable and chose not to.	

- Say, "**I am sorry for these and all of my sins**."
- Listen to the priest and pray an **Act of Contrition**:

   Act of Contrition - My God, I am sorry for my sins with all my heart. In choosing to do wrong and failing to do good, I have sinned against You whom I should love above all things. I firmly intend, with Your help, to do penance, to sin no more, and to avoid whatever leads me to sin. Our Savior Jesus Christ suffered and died for us. In His Name, my God, have mercy. Amen.

   Or

   Act of Contrition: O my God, I am heartily sorry for having offended You and I detest all my sins, because I dread the loss of heaven and the pains of hell. But most of all because I have offended You, my God, who are all good and deserving of all my love. I firmly resolve with the help of Your grace, to confess my sins, to do penance and to amend my life. Amen.

- Priest will say words of absolution (forgiveness). Make the Sign of the Cross.
- If he closes by saying, "Give thanks to the Lord for He is good," answer, **"For His mercy endures forever."**
- Perform your penance.
- Thank God.

"The confession of evil works is the first beginning of good works."—*St. Augustine*

Today's Date: _____

Before Confession:
- Pray, "Come Holy Spirit" and make an Examination of Conscience. (Chapter 2)
- Pray for your confessor.

During Confession
- Priest welcomes you. Make the Sign of the Cross.
- Say "**Bless me Father, for I have sinned, this is my First Confession,**" or "**Bless me Father, for I have sinned, my last Confession was _____ (days, weeks, months) ago.**"
- Tell the priest your sins below:

✔	The Lord says, "You Shall Love the Lord Your God with your whole heart."	# Of Times?
	I did not obey God right away.	
	I doubted God's love for me.	
	I did not use all the graces God gave me to become closer to Him.	
	I did not pray my daily prayers (morning, evening, meals).	
	I put other things before God (friends, toys, games, and money).	
	I did not try to do my best for Jesus, even when I had to do things I didn't want to.	
	I spent money unwisely.	
	I placed my faith things other than God (good luck charms, etc.)	
	I said God's name in anger or frustration and / or spoke disrespectfully of God or Our Lady.	
	I used bad words (swear words).	
	I did not show reverence toward sacred persons, places, and things (e.g., the Pope, Bishop, priests, nuns, brothers, crucifixes, sacramentals, etc.).	
	I missed Mass on purpose on a Sunday or Holy Day of Obligation.	
	I was late for Mass or my behavior played a factor in our being late for Mass.	
	I did not abstain or fast according to Church teaching (one hour before receiving Jesus in Eucharist, no meat on Friday during Lent, etc.).	
	I laughed or distracted others in church.	
✔	The Lord Says, "You shall love your neighbor as yourself,"	
	I did not give my parent, guardian, or teacher right-away obedience.	
	I was disrespectful to my parent, guardian, or teacher.	

"The confession of evil works is the first beginning of good works."—St. Augustine

I did not do my chores without grumbling or needing to be nagged.	
I spoke uncharitably to my parent, guardian, teacher, friend, sibling, etc.	
I lied.	
I took something that did not belong to me.	
I teased someone.	
I hurt someone.	
I did not treat my body, a temple of the Holy Spirit, with respect (ate too much, dressed immodestly, avoided exercise, etc.).	
I did not respect other's personal space.	
I said unkind words to or about someone else.	
I became envious of something someone else has or has achieved.	
I became angry or envious and did not handle my feelings in a positive way.	
I was prideful or boastful.	
I could have helped somebody and chose not to.	
I could have shared and chose not to.	
I could have been charitable and chose not to.	

- Say, "**I am sorry for these and all of my sins.**"
- Listen to the priest and pray an **Act of Contrition**:

  Act of Contrition - My God, I am sorry for my sins with all my heart. In choosing to do wrong and failing to do good, I have sinned against You whom I should love above all things. I firmly intend, with Your help, to do penance, to sin no more, and to avoid whatever leads me to sin. Our Savior Jesus Christ suffered and died for us. In His Name, my God, have mercy. Amen.

  Or

  Act of Contrition: O my God, I am heartily sorry for having offended You and I detest all my sins, because I dread the loss of heaven and the pains of hell. But most of all because I have offended You, my God, who are all good and deserving of all my love. I firmly resolve with the help of Your grace, to confess my sins, to do penance and to amend my life. Amen.

- Priest will say words of absolution (forgiveness). Make the Sign of the Cross.
- If he closes by saying, "Give thanks to the Lord for He is good," answer, "**For His mercy endures forever.**"
- Perform your penance.
- Thank God.

"The confession of evil works is the first beginning of good works."—St. Augustine

Today's Date: _____

Before Confession:
- Pray, "Come Holy Spirit" and make an Examination of Conscience. (Chapter 2)
- Pray for your confessor.

During Confession
- Priest welcomes you. Make the Sign of the Cross.
- Say **"Bless me Father, for I have sinned, this is my First Confession,"** or **"Bless me Father, for I have sinned, my last Confession was _____ (days, weeks, months) ago."**
- Tell the priest your sins below:

✔	The Lord says, "You Shall Love the Lord Your God with your whole heart."	# Of Times?
	I did not obey God right away.	
	I doubted God's love for me.	
	I did not use all the graces God gave me to become closer to Him.	
	I did not pray my daily prayers (morning, evening, meals).	
	I put other things before God (friends, toys, games, and money).	
	I did not try to do my best for Jesus, even when I had to do things I didn't want to.	
	I spent money unwisely.	
	I placed my faith things other than God (good luck charms, etc.)	
	I said God's name in anger or frustration and / or spoke disrespectfully of God or Our Lady.	
	I used bad words (swear words).	
	I did not show reverence toward sacred persons, places, and things (e.g., the Pope, Bishop, priests, nuns, brothers, crucifixes, sacramentals, etc.).	
	I missed Mass on purpose on a Sunday or Holy Day of Obligation.	
	I was late for Mass or my behavior played a factor in our being late for Mass.	
	I did not abstain or fast according to Church teaching (one hour before receiving Jesus in Eucharist, no meat on Friday during Lent, etc.).	
	I laughed or distracted others in church.	
✔	The Lord Says, "You shall love your neighbor as yourself,"	
	I did not give my parent, guardian, or teacher right-away obedience.	
	I was disrespectful to my parent, guardian, or teacher.	

"The confession of evil works is the first beginning of good works."—St. Augustine

I did not do my chores without grumbling or needing to be nagged.	
I spoke uncharitably to my parent, guardian, teacher, friend, sibling, etc.	
I lied.	
I took something that did not belong to me.	
I teased someone.	
I hurt someone.	
I did not treat my body, a temple of the Holy Spirit, with respect (ate too much, dressed immodestly, avoided exercise, etc.).	
I did not respect other's personal space.	
I said unkind words to or about someone else.	
I became envious of something someone else has or has achieved.	
I became angry or envious and did not handle my feelings in a positive way.	
I was prideful or boastful.	
I could have helped somebody and chose not to.	
I could have shared and chose not to.	
I could have been charitable and chose not to.	

- Say, "**I am sorry for these and all of my sins.**"
- Listen to the priest and pray an **Act of Contrition**:
  Act of Contrition - My God, I am sorry for my sins with all my heart. In choosing to do wrong and failing to do good, I have sinned against You whom I should love above all things. I firmly intend, with Your help, to do penance, to sin no more, and to avoid whatever leads me to sin. Our Savior Jesus Christ suffered and died for us. In His Name, my God, have mercy. Amen.
  Or
  Act of Contrition: O my God, I am heartily sorry for having offended You and I detest all my sins, because I dread the loss of heaven and the pains of hell. But most of all because I have offended You, my God, who are all good and deserving of all my love. I firmly resolve with the help of Your grace, to confess my sins, to do penance and to amend my life. Amen.

- Priest will say words of absolution (forgiveness). Make the Sign of the Cross.
- If he closes by saying, "Give thanks to the Lord for He is good," answer, **"For His mercy endures forever."**
- Perform your penance.
- Thank God.

"The confession of evil works is the first beginning of good works."—*St. Augustine*

Today's Date: _____

Before Confession:
- Pray, "Come Holy Spirit" and make an Examination of Conscience. (Chapter 2)
- Pray for your confessor.

During Confession
- Priest welcomes you. Make the Sign of the Cross.
- Say "**Bless me Father, for I have sinned, this is my First Confession,**" or "**Bless me Father, for I have sinned, my last Confession was _____ (days, weeks, months) ago.**"
- Tell the priest your sins below:

✔ The Lord says, "You Shall Love the Lord Your God with your whole heart."	# Of Times?
I did not obey God right away.	
I doubted God's love for me.	
I did not use all the graces God gave me to become closer to Him.	
I did not pray my daily prayers (morning, evening, meals).	
I put other things before God (friends, toys, games, and money).	
I did not try to do my best for Jesus, even when I had to do things I didn't want to.	
I spent money unwisely.	
I placed my faith things other than God (good luck charms, etc.)	
I said God's name in anger or frustration and / or spoke disrespectfully of God or Our Lady.	
I used bad words (swear words).	
I did not show reverence toward sacred persons, places, and things (e.g., the Pope, Bishop, priests, nuns, brothers, crucifixes, sacramentals, etc.).	
I missed Mass on purpose on a Sunday or Holy Day of Obligation.	
I was late for Mass or my behavior played a factor in our being late for Mass.	
I did not abstain or fast according to Church teaching (one hour before receiving Jesus in Eucharist, no meat on Friday during Lent, etc.).	
I laughed or distracted others in church.	
✔ The Lord Says, "You shall love your neighbor as yourself,"	
I did not give my parent, guardian, or teacher right-away obedience.	
I was disrespectful to my parent, guardian, or teacher.	

"The confession of evil works is the first beginning of good works."—St. Augustine

I did not do my chores without grumbling or needing to be nagged.	
I spoke uncharitably to my parent, guardian, teacher, friend, sibling, etc.	
I lied.	
I took something that did not belong to me.	
I teased someone.	
I hurt someone.	
I did not treat my body, a temple of the Holy Spirit, with respect (ate too much, dressed immodestly, avoided exercise, etc.).	
I did not respect other's personal space.	
I said unkind words to or about someone else.	
I became envious of something someone else has or has achieved.	
I became angry or envious and did not handle my feelings in a positive way.	
I was prideful or boastful.	
I could have helped somebody and chose not to.	
I could have shared and chose not to.	
I could have been charitable and chose not to.	

- Say, "**I am sorry for these and all of my sins**."
- Listen to the priest and pray an **Act of Contrition**:
  Act of Contrition - My God, I am sorry for my sins with all my heart. In choosing to do wrong and failing to do good, I have sinned against You whom I should love above all things. I firmly intend, with Your help, to do penance, to sin no more, and to avoid whatever leads me to sin. Our Savior Jesus Christ suffered and died for us. In His Name, my God, have mercy. Amen.
  Or
  Act of Contrition: O my God, I am heartily sorry for having offended You and I detest all my sins, because I dread the loss of heaven and the pains of hell. But most of all because I have offended You, my God, who are all good and deserving of all my love. I firmly resolve with the help of Your grace, to confess my sins, to do penance and to amend my life. Amen.

- Priest will say words of absolution (forgiveness). Make the Sign of the Cross.
- If he closes by saying, "Give thanks to the Lord for He is good," answer, "**For His mercy endures forever.**"
- Perform your penance.
- Thank God.

"The confession of evil works is the first beginning of good works."—St. Augustine

Today's Date: _____

Before Confession:

- Pray, "Come Holy Spirit" and make an Examination of Conscience. (Chapter 2)
- Pray for your confessor.

During Confession

- Priest welcomes you. Make the Sign of the Cross.
- Say "**Bless me Father, for I have sinned, this is my First Confession,**" or "**Bless me Father, for I have sinned, my last Confession was** _____ (**days, weeks, months) ago.**"
- Tell the priest your sins below:

✔	The Lord says, "You Shall Love the Lord Your God with your whole heart."	# Of Times?
	I did not obey God right away.	
	I doubted God's love for me.	
	I did not use all the graces God gave me to become closer to Him.	
	I did not pray my daily prayers (morning, evening, meals).	
	I put other things before God (friends, toys, games, and money).	
	I did not try to do my best for Jesus, even when I had to do things I didn't want to.	
	I spent money unwisely.	
	I placed my faith things other than God (good luck charms, etc.)	
	I said God's name in anger or frustration and / or spoke disrespectfully of God or Our Lady.	
	I used bad words (swear words).	
	I did not show reverence toward sacred persons, places, and things (e.g., the Pope, Bishop, priests, nuns, brothers, crucifixes, sacramentals, etc.).	
	I missed Mass on purpose on a Sunday or Holy Day of Obligation.	
	I was late for Mass or my behavior played a factor in our being late for Mass.	
	I did not abstain or fast according to Church teaching (one hour before receiving Jesus in Eucharist, no meat on Friday during Lent, etc.).	
	I laughed or distracted others in church.	
✔	The Lord Says, "You shall love your neighbor as yourself,"	
	I did not give my parent, guardian, or teacher right-away obedience.	
	I was disrespectful to my parent, guardian, or teacher.	

"The confession of evil works is the first beginning of good works."—*St. Augustine*

I did not do my chores without grumbling or needing to be nagged.	
I spoke uncharitably to my parent, guardian, teacher, friend, sibling, etc.	
I lied.	
I took something that did not belong to me.	
I teased someone.	
I hurt someone.	
I did not treat my body, a temple of the Holy Spirit, with respect (ate too much, dressed immodestly, avoided exercise, etc.).	
I did not respect other's personal space.	
I said unkind words to or about someone else.	
I became envious of something someone else has or has achieved.	
I became angry or envious and did not handle my feelings in a positive way.	
I was prideful or boastful.	
I could have helped somebody and chose not to.	
I could have shared and chose not to.	
I could have been charitable and chose not to.	

- Say, "**I am sorry for these and all of my sins.**"
- Listen to the priest and pray an **Act of Contrition**:
  Act of Contrition - My God, I am sorry for my sins with all my heart. In choosing to do wrong and failing to do good, I have sinned against You whom I should love above all things. I firmly intend, with Your help, to do penance, to sin no more, and to avoid whatever leads me to sin. Our Savior Jesus Christ suffered and died for us. In His Name, my God, have mercy. Amen.
  Or
  Act of Contrition: O my God, I am heartily sorry for having offended You and I detest all my sins, because I dread the loss of heaven and the pains of hell. But most of all because I have offended You, my God, who are all good and deserving of all my love. I firmly resolve with the help of Your grace, to confess my sins, to do penance and to amend my life. Amen.

- Priest will say words of absolution (forgiveness). Make the Sign of the Cross.
- If he closes by saying, "Give thanks to the Lord for He is good," answer, "**For His mercy endures forever.**"
- Perform your penance.
- Thank God.

"The confession of evil works is the first beginning of good works."—*St. Augustine*

Today's Date: _____

Before Confession:

- Pray, "Come Holy Spirit" and make an Examination of Conscience. (Chapter 2)
- Pray for your confessor.

During Confession

- Priest welcomes you. Make the Sign of the Cross.
- Say "**Bless me Father, for I have sinned, this is my First Confession,**" or "**Bless me Father, for I have sinned, my last Confession was** _____ **(days, weeks, months) ago.**"
- Tell the priest your sins below:

✔	The Lord says, "You Shall Love the Lord Your God with your whole heart."	# Of Times?
	I did not obey God right away.	
	I doubted God's love for me.	
	I did not use all the graces God gave me to become closer to Him.	
	I did not pray my daily prayers (morning, evening, meals).	
	I put other things before God (friends, toys, games, and money).	
	I did not try to do my best for Jesus, even when I had to do things I didn't want to.	
	I spent money unwisely.	
	I placed my faith things other than God (good luck charms, etc.)	
	I said God's name in anger or frustration and / or spoke disrespectfully of God or Our Lady.	
	I used bad words (swear words).	
	I did not show reverence toward sacred persons, places, and things (e.g., the Pope, Bishop, priests, nuns, brothers, crucifixes, sacramentals, etc.).	
	I missed Mass on purpose on a Sunday or Holy Day of Obligation.	
	I was late for Mass or my behavior played a factor in our being late for Mass.	
	I did not abstain or fast according to Church teaching (one hour before receiving Jesus in Eucharist, no meat on Friday during Lent, etc.).	
	I laughed or distracted others in church.	
✔	The Lord Says, "You shall love your neighbor as yourself,"	
	I did not give my parent, guardian, or teacher right-away obedience.	
	I was disrespectful to my parent, guardian, or teacher.	

"The confession of evil works is the first beginning of good works."—St. Augustine

I did not do my chores without grumbling or needing to be nagged.	
I spoke uncharitably to my parent, guardian, teacher, friend, sibling, etc.	
I lied.	
I took something that did not belong to me.	
I teased someone.	
I hurt someone.	
I did not treat my body, a temple of the Holy Spirit, with respect (ate too much, dressed immodestly, avoided exercise, etc.).	
I did not respect other's personal space.	
I said unkind words to or about someone else.	
I became envious of something someone else has or has achieved.	
I became angry or envious and did not handle my feelings in a positive way.	
I was prideful or boastful.	
I could have helped somebody and chose not to.	
I could have shared and chose not to.	
I could have been charitable and chose not to.	

- Say, "**I am sorry for these and all of my sins.**"
- Listen to the priest and pray an **Act of Contrition**:
  Act of Contrition - My God, I am sorry for my sins with all my heart. In choosing to do wrong and failing to do good, I have sinned against You whom I should love above all things. I firmly intend, with Your help, to do penance, to sin no more, and to avoid whatever leads me to sin. Our Savior Jesus Christ suffered and died for us. In His Name, my God, have mercy. Amen.
  Or
  Act of Contrition: O my God, I am heartily sorry for having offended You and I detest all my sins, because I dread the loss of heaven and the pains of hell. But most of all because I have offended You, my God, who are all good and deserving of all my love. I firmly resolve with the help of Your grace, to confess my sins, to do penance and to amend my life. Amen.

- Priest will say words of absolution (forgiveness). Make the Sign of the Cross.
- If he closes by saying, "Give thanks to the Lord for He is good," answer, **"For His mercy endures forever."**
- Perform your penance.
- Thank God.

"The confession of evil works is the first beginning of good works."—St. Augustine

Today's Date: _____

Before Confession:

- Pray, "Come Holy Spirit" and make an Examination of Conscience. (Chapter 2)
- Pray for your confessor.

During Confession

- Priest welcomes you. Make the Sign of the Cross.
- Say "**Bless me Father, for I have sinned, this is my First Confession,**" or "**Bless me Father, for I have sinned, my last Confession was _____ (days, weeks, months) ago.**"
- Tell the priest your sins below:

✔	The Lord says, "You Shall Love the Lord Your God with your whole heart."	# Of Times?
	I did not obey God right away.	
	I doubted God's love for me.	
	I did not use all the graces God gave me to become closer to Him.	
	I did not pray my daily prayers (morning, evening, meals).	
	I put other things before God (friends, toys, games, and money).	
	I did not try to do my best for Jesus, even when I had to do things I didn't want to.	
	I spent money unwisely.	
	I placed my faith things other than God (good luck charms, etc.)	
	I said God's name in anger or frustration and / or spoke disrespectfully of God or Our Lady.	
	I used bad words (swear words).	
	I did not show reverence toward sacred persons, places, and things (e.g., the Pope, Bishop, priests, nuns, brothers, crucifixes, sacramentals, etc.).	
	I missed Mass on purpose on a Sunday or Holy Day of Obligation.	
	I was late for Mass or my behavior played a factor in our being late for Mass.	
	I did not abstain or fast according to Church teaching (one hour before receiving Jesus in Eucharist, no meat on Friday during Lent, etc.).	
	I laughed or distracted others in church.	
✔	The Lord Says, "You shall love your neighbor as yourself,"	
	I did not give my parent, guardian, or teacher right-away obedience.	
	I was disrespectful to my parent, guardian, or teacher.	

"The confession of evil works is the first beginning of good works."—*St. Augustine*

I did not do my chores without grumbling or needing to be nagged.	
I spoke uncharitably to my parent, guardian, teacher, friend, sibling, etc.	
I lied.	
I took something that did not belong to me.	
I teased someone.	
I hurt someone.	
I did not treat my body, a temple of the Holy Spirit, with respect (ate too much, dressed immodestly, avoided exercise, etc.).	
I did not respect other's personal space.	
I said unkind words to or about someone else.	
I became envious of something someone else has or has achieved.	
I became angry or envious and did not handle my feelings in a positive way.	
I was prideful or boastful.	
I could have helped somebody and chose not to.	
I could have shared and chose not to.	
I could have been charitable and chose not to.	

- Say, "**I am sorry for these and all of my sins.**"
- Listen to the priest and pray an **Act of Contrition**:
  Act of Contrition - My God, I am sorry for my sins with all my heart. In choosing to do wrong and failing to do good, I have sinned against You whom I should love above all things. I firmly intend, with Your help, to do penance, to sin no more, and to avoid whatever leads me to sin. Our Savior Jesus Christ suffered and died for us. In His Name, my God, have mercy. Amen.
  Or
  Act of Contrition: O my God, I am heartily sorry for having offended You and I detest all my sins, because I dread the loss of heaven and the pains of hell. But most of all because I have offended You, my God, who are all good and deserving of all my love. I firmly resolve with the help of Your grace, to confess my sins, to do penance and to amend my life. Amen.

- Priest will say words of absolution (forgiveness). Make the Sign of the Cross.
- If he closes by saying, "Give thanks to the Lord for He is good," answer, **"For His mercy endures forever."**
- Perform your penance.
- Thank God.

"The confession of evil works is the first beginning of good works."—*St. Augustine*

Today's Date: _____

Before Confession:

- Pray, "Come Holy Spirit" and make an Examination of Conscience. (Chapter 2)
- Pray for your confessor.

During Confession

- Priest welcomes you. Make the Sign of the Cross.
- Say "**Bless me Father, for I have sinned, this is my First Confession,**" or "**Bless me Father, for I have sinned, my last Confession was** _____ **(days, weeks, months) ago.**"
- Tell the priest your sins below:

✔ The Lord says, "You Shall Love the Lord Your God with your whole heart."	# Of Times?
I did not obey God right away.	
I doubted God's love for me.	
I did not use all the graces God gave me to become closer to Him.	
I did not pray my daily prayers (morning, evening, meals).	
I put other things before God (friends, toys, games, and money).	
I did not try to do my best for Jesus, even when I had to do things I didn't want to.	
I spent money unwisely.	
I placed my faith things other than God (good luck charms, etc.)	
I said God's name in anger or frustration and / or spoke disrespectfully of God or Our Lady.	
I used bad words (swear words).	
I did not show reverence toward sacred persons, places, and things (e.g., the Pope, Bishop, priests, nuns, brothers, crucifixes, sacramentals, etc.).	
I missed Mass on purpose on a Sunday or Holy Day of Obligation.	
I was late for Mass or my behavior played a factor in our being late for Mass.	
I did not abstain or fast according to Church teaching (one hour before receiving Jesus in Eucharist, no meat on Friday during Lent, etc.).	
I laughed or distracted others in church.	
✔ The Lord Says, "You shall love your neighbor as yourself,"	
I did not give my parent, guardian, or teacher right-away obedience.	
I was disrespectful to my parent, guardian, or teacher.	

"The confession of evil works is the first beginning of good works."—St. Augustine

I did not do my chores without grumbling or needing to be nagged.	
I spoke uncharitably to my parent, guardian, teacher, friend, sibling, etc.	
I lied.	
I took something that did not belong to me.	
I teased someone.	
I hurt someone.	
I did not treat my body, a temple of the Holy Spirit, with respect (ate too much, dressed immodestly, avoided exercise, etc.).	
I did not respect other's personal space.	
I said unkind words to or about someone else.	
I became envious of something someone else has or has achieved.	
I became angry or envious and did not handle my feelings in a positive way.	
I was prideful or boastful.	
I could have helped somebody and chose not to.	
I could have shared and chose not to.	
I could have been charitable and chose not to.	

- Say, "**I am sorry for these and all of my sins.**"
- Listen to the priest and pray an **Act of Contrition**:

  Act of Contrition - My God, I am sorry for my sins with all my heart. In choosing to do wrong and failing to do good, I have sinned against You whom I should love above all things. I firmly intend, with Your help, to do penance, to sin no more, and to avoid whatever leads me to sin. Our Savior Jesus Christ suffered and died for us. In His Name, my God, have mercy. Amen.

  Or

  Act of Contrition: O my God, I am heartily sorry for having offended You and I detest all my sins, because I dread the loss of heaven and the pains of hell. But most of all because I have offended You, my God, who are all good and deserving of all my love. I firmly resolve with the help of Your grace, to confess my sins, to do penance and to amend my life. Amen.

- Priest will say words of absolution (forgiveness). Make the Sign of the Cross.
- If he closes by saying, "Give thanks to the Lord for He is good," answer, "**For His mercy endures forever.**"
- Perform your penance.
- Thank God.

"The confession of evil works is the first beginning of good works."—St. Augustine

Today's Date: _____

Before Confession:

- Pray, "Come Holy Spirit" and make an Examination of Conscience. (Chapter 2)
- Pray for your confessor.

During Confession

- Priest welcomes you. Make the Sign of the Cross.
- Say **"Bless me Father, for I have sinned, this is my First Confession,"** or **"Bless me Father, for I have sinned, my last Confession was _____ (days, weeks, months) ago."**
- Tell the priest your sins below:

✓ The Lord says, "You Shall Love the Lord Your God with your whole heart."	# Of Times?
I did not obey God right away.	
I doubted God's love for me.	
I did not use all the graces God gave me to become closer to Him.	
I did not pray my daily prayers (morning, evening, meals).	
I put other things before God (friends, toys, games, and money).	
I did not try to do my best for Jesus, even when I had to do things I didn't want to.	
I spent money unwisely.	
I placed my faith things other than God (good luck charms, etc.)	
I said God's name in anger or frustration and / or spoke disrespectfully of God or Our Lady.	
I used bad words (swear words).	
I did not show reverence toward sacred persons, places, and things (e.g., the Pope, Bishop, priests, nuns, brothers, crucifixes, sacramentals, etc.).	
I missed Mass on purpose on a Sunday or Holy Day of Obligation.	
I was late for Mass or my behavior played a factor in our being late for Mass.	
I did not abstain or fast according to Church teaching (one hour before receiving Jesus in Eucharist, no meat on Friday during Lent, etc.).	
I laughed or distracted others in church.	
✓ The Lord Says, "You shall love your neighbor as yourself,"	
I did not give my parent, guardian, or teacher right-away obedience.	
I was disrespectful to my parent, guardian, or teacher.	

"The confession of evil works is the first beginning of good works."—St. Augustine

I did not do my chores without grumbling or needing to be nagged.	
I spoke uncharitably to my parent, guardian, teacher, friend, sibling, etc.	
I lied.	
I took something that did not belong to me.	
I teased someone.	
I hurt someone.	
I did not treat my body, a temple of the Holy Spirit, with respect (ate too much, dressed immodestly, avoided exercise, etc.).	
I did not respect other's personal space.	
I said unkind words to or about someone else.	
I became envious of something someone else has or has achieved.	
I became angry or envious and did not handle my feelings in a positive way.	
I was prideful or boastful.	
I could have helped somebody and chose not to.	
I could have shared and chose not to.	
I could have been charitable and chose not to.	

- Say, "**I am sorry for these and all of my sins.**"
- Listen to the priest and pray an **Act of Contrition**:
  Act of Contrition - My God, I am sorry for my sins with all my heart. In choosing to do wrong and failing to do good, I have sinned against You whom I should love above all things. I firmly intend, with Your help, to do penance, to sin no more, and to avoid whatever leads me to sin. Our Savior Jesus Christ suffered and died for us. In His Name, my God, have mercy. Amen.
  Or
  Act of Contrition: O my God, I am heartily sorry for having offended You and I detest all my sins, because I dread the loss of heaven and the pains of hell. But most of all because I have offended You, my God, who are all good and deserving of all my love. I firmly resolve with the help of Your grace, to confess my sins, to do penance and to amend my life. Amen.

- Priest will say words of absolution (forgiveness). Make the Sign of the Cross.
- If he closes by saying, "Give thanks to the Lord for He is good," answer, **"For His mercy endures forever."**
- Perform your penance.
- Thank God.

"The confession of evil works is the first beginning of good works."—St. Augustine

Today's Date: _____

Before Confession:
- Pray, "Come Holy Spirit" and make an Examination of Conscience. (Chapter 2)
- Pray for your confessor.

During Confession
- Priest welcomes you. Make the Sign of the Cross.
- Say **"Bless me Father, for I have sinned, this is my First Confession,"** or **"Bless me Father, for I have sinned, my last Confession was _____ (days, weeks, months) ago."**
- Tell the priest your sins below:

✔ The Lord says, "You Shall Love the Lord Your God with your whole heart."	# Of Times?
I did not obey God right away.	
I doubted God's love for me.	
I did not use all the graces God gave me to become closer to Him.	
I did not pray my daily prayers (morning, evening, meals).	
I put other things before God (friends, toys, games, and money).	
I did not try to do my best for Jesus, even when I had to do things I didn't want to.	
I spent money unwisely.	
I placed my faith things other than God (good luck charms, etc.)	
I said God's name in anger or frustration and / or spoke disrespectfully of God or Our Lady.	
I used bad words (swear words).	
I did not show reverence toward sacred persons, places, and things (e.g., the Pope, Bishop, priests, nuns, brothers, crucifixes, sacramentals, etc.).	
I missed Mass on purpose on a Sunday or Holy Day of Obligation.	
I was late for Mass or my behavior played a factor in our being late for Mass.	
I did not abstain or fast according to Church teaching (one hour before receiving Jesus in Eucharist, no meat on Friday during Lent, etc.).	
I laughed or distracted others in church.	
✔ The Lord Says, "You shall love your neighbor as yourself,"	
I did not give my parent, guardian, or teacher right-away obedience.	
I was disrespectful to my parent, guardian, or teacher.	

"The confession of evil works is the first beginning of good works."—St. Augustine

I did not do my chores without grumbling or needing to be nagged.	
I spoke uncharitably to my parent, guardian, teacher, friend, sibling, etc.	
I lied.	
I took something that did not belong to me.	
I teased someone.	
I hurt someone.	
I did not treat my body, a temple of the Holy Spirit, with respect (ate too much, dressed immodestly, avoided exercise, etc.).	
I did not respect other's personal space.	
I said unkind words to or about someone else.	
I became envious of something someone else has or has achieved.	
I became angry or envious and did not handle my feelings in a positive way.	
I was prideful or boastful.	
I could have helped somebody and chose not to.	
I could have shared and chose not to.	
I could have been charitable and chose not to.	

- Say, "**I am sorry for these and all of my sins.**"
- Listen to the priest and pray an **Act of Contrition**:
  Act of Contrition - My God, I am sorry for my sins with all my heart. In choosing to do wrong and failing to do good, I have sinned against You whom I should love above all things. I firmly intend, with Your help, to do penance, to sin no more, and to avoid whatever leads me to sin. Our Savior Jesus Christ suffered and died for us. In His Name, my God, have mercy. Amen.
  Or
  Act of Contrition: O my God, I am heartily sorry for having offended You and I detest all my sins, because I dread the loss of heaven and the pains of hell. But most of all because I have offended You, my God, who are all good and deserving of all my love. I firmly resolve with the help of Your grace, to confess my sins, to do penance and to amend my life. Amen.

- Priest will say words of absolution (forgiveness). Make the Sign of the Cross.
- If he closes by saying, "Give thanks to the Lord for He is good," answer, **"For His mercy endures forever."**
- Perform your penance.
- Thank God.

"The confession of evil works is the first beginning of good works."—St. Augustine

Today's Date: _____

Before Confession:
- Pray, "Come Holy Spirit" and make an Examination of Conscience. (Chapter 2)
- Pray for your confessor.

During Confession
- Priest welcomes you. Make the Sign of the Cross.
- Say "**Bless me Father, for I have sinned, this is my First Confession,**" or "**Bless me Father, for I have sinned, my last Confession was _____ (days, weeks, months) ago.**"
- Tell the priest your sins below:

✔	The Lord says, "You Shall Love the Lord Your God with your whole heart."	# Of Times?
	I did not obey God right away.	
	I doubted God's love for me.	
	I did not use all the graces God gave me to become closer to Him.	
	I did not pray my daily prayers (morning, evening, meals).	
	I put other things before God (friends, toys, games, and money).	
	I did not try to do my best for Jesus, even when I had to do things I didn't want to.	
	I spent money unwisely.	
	I placed my faith things other than God (good luck charms, etc.)	
	I said God's name in anger or frustration and / or spoke disrespectfully of God or Our Lady.	
	I used bad words (swear words).	
	I did not show reverence toward sacred persons, places, and things (e.g., the Pope, Bishop, priests, nuns, brothers, crucifixes, sacramentals, etc.).	
	I missed Mass on purpose on a Sunday or Holy Day of Obligation.	
	I was late for Mass or my behavior played a factor in our being late for Mass.	
	I did not abstain or fast according to Church teaching (one hour before receiving Jesus in Eucharist, no meat on Friday during Lent, etc.).	
	I laughed or distracted others in church.	
✔	The Lord Says, "You shall love your neighbor as yourself,"	
	I did not give my parent, guardian, or teacher right-away obedience.	
	I was disrespectful to my parent, guardian, or teacher.	

"The confession of evil works is the first beginning of good works."—St. Augustine

I did not do my chores without grumbling or needing to be nagged.	
I spoke uncharitably to my parent, guardian, teacher, friend, sibling, etc.	
I lied.	
I took something that did not belong to me.	
I teased someone.	
I hurt someone.	
I did not treat my body, a temple of the Holy Spirit, with respect (ate too much, dressed immodestly, avoided exercise, etc.).	
I did not respect other's personal space.	
I said unkind words to or about someone else.	
I became envious of something someone else has or has achieved.	
I became angry or envious and did not handle my feelings in a positive way.	
I was prideful or boastful.	
I could have helped somebody and chose not to.	
I could have shared and chose not to.	
I could have been charitable and chose not to.	

- Say, "**I am sorry for these and all of my sins.**"
- Listen to the priest and pray an **Act of Contrition**:
  Act of Contrition - My God, I am sorry for my sins with all my heart. In choosing to do wrong and failing to do good, I have sinned against You whom I should love above all things. I firmly intend, with Your help, to do penance, to sin no more, and to avoid whatever leads me to sin. Our Savior Jesus Christ suffered and died for us. In His Name, my God, have mercy. Amen.
  Or
  Act of Contrition: O my God, I am heartily sorry for having offended You and I detest all my sins, because I dread the loss of heaven and the pains of hell. But most of all because I have offended You, my God, who are all good and deserving of all my love. I firmly resolve with the help of Your grace, to confess my sins, to do penance and to amend my life. Amen.

- Priest will say words of absolution (forgiveness). Make the Sign of the Cross.
- If he closes by saying, "Give thanks to the Lord for He is good," answer, **"For His mercy endures forever."**
- Perform your penance.
- Thank God.

"The confession of evil works is the first beginning of good works."—St. Augustine

Today's Date: _____

Before Confession:

- Pray, "Come Holy Spirit" and make an Examination of Conscience. (Chapter 2)
- Pray for your confessor.

During Confession

- Priest welcomes you. Make the Sign of the Cross.
- Say "**Bless me Father, for I have sinned, this is my First Confession**," or "**Bless me Father, for I have sinned, my last Confession was _____ (days, weeks, months) ago.**"
- Tell the priest your sins below:

✓ The Lord says, "You Shall Love the Lord Your God with your whole heart."	# Of Times?
I did not obey God right away.	
I doubted God's love for me.	
I did not use all the graces God gave me to become closer to Him.	
I did not pray my daily prayers (morning, evening, meals).	
I put other things before God (friends, toys, games, and money).	
I did not try to do my best for Jesus, even when I had to do things I didn't want to.	
I spent money unwisely.	
I placed my faith things other than God (good luck charms, etc.)	
I said God's name in anger or frustration and / or spoke disrespectfully of God or Our Lady.	
I used bad words (swear words).	
I did not show reverence toward sacred persons, places, and things (e.g., the Pope, Bishop, priests, nuns, brothers, crucifixes, sacramentals, etc.).	
I missed Mass on purpose on a Sunday or Holy Day of Obligation.	
I was late for Mass or my behavior played a factor in our being late for Mass.	
I did not abstain or fast according to Church teaching (one hour before receiving Jesus in Eucharist, no meat on Friday during Lent, etc.).	
I laughed or distracted others in church.	
✓ The Lord Says, "You shall love your neighbor as yourself,"	
I did not give my parent, guardian, or teacher right-away obedience.	
I was disrespectful to my parent, guardian, or teacher.	

"The confession of evil works is the first beginning of good works."—St. Augustine

I did not do my chores without grumbling or needing to be nagged.	
I spoke uncharitably to my parent, guardian, teacher, friend, sibling, etc.	
I lied.	
I took something that did not belong to me.	
I teased someone.	
I hurt someone.	
I did not treat my body, a temple of the Holy Spirit, with respect (ate too much, dressed immodestly, avoided exercise, etc.).	
I did not respect other's personal space.	
I said unkind words to or about someone else.	
I became envious of something someone else has or has achieved.	
I became angry or envious and did not handle my feelings in a positive way.	
I was prideful or boastful.	
I could have helped somebody and chose not to.	
I could have shared and chose not to.	
I could have been charitable and chose not to.	

- Say, "**I am sorry for these and all of my sins.**"
- Listen to the priest and pray an **Act of Contrition**:
  Act of Contrition - My God, I am sorry for my sins with all my heart. In choosing to do wrong and failing to do good, I have sinned against You whom I should love above all things. I firmly intend, with Your help, to do penance, to sin no more, and to avoid whatever leads me to sin. Our Savior Jesus Christ suffered and died for us. In His Name, my God, have mercy. Amen.
  Or
  Act of Contrition: O my God, I am heartily sorry for having offended You and I detest all my sins, because I dread the loss of heaven and the pains of hell. But most of all because I have offended You, my God, who are all good and deserving of all my love. I firmly resolve with the help of Your grace, to confess my sins, to do penance and to amend my life. Amen.

- Priest will say words of absolution (forgiveness). Make the Sign of the Cross.
- If he closes by saying, "Give thanks to the Lord for He is good," answer, **"For His mercy endures forever."**
- Perform your penance.
- Thank God.

"The confession of evil works is the first beginning of good works."—St. Augustine

Today's Date: _____

Before Confession:

- Pray, "Come Holy Spirit" and make an Examination of Conscience. (Chapter 2)
- Pray for your confessor.

During Confession

- Priest welcomes you. Make the Sign of the Cross.
- Say "**Bless me Father, for I have sinned, this is my First Confession,**" or "**Bless me Father, for I have sinned, my last Confession was _____ (days, weeks, months) ago.**"
- Tell the priest your sins below:

✔	The Lord says, "You Shall Love the Lord Your God with your whole heart."	# Of Times?
	I did not obey God right away.	
	I doubted God's love for me.	
	I did not use all the graces God gave me to become closer to Him.	
	I did not pray my daily prayers (morning, evening, meals).	
	I put other things before God (friends, toys, games, and money).	
	I did not try to do my best for Jesus, even when I had to do things I didn't want to.	
	I spent money unwisely.	
	I placed my faith things other than God (good luck charms, etc.)	
	I said God's name in anger or frustration and / or spoke disrespectfully of God or Our Lady.	
	I used bad words (swear words).	
	I did not show reverence toward sacred persons, places, and things (e.g., the Pope, Bishop, priests, nuns, brothers, crucifixes, sacramentals, etc.).	
	I missed Mass on purpose on a Sunday or Holy Day of Obligation.	
	I was late for Mass or my behavior played a factor in our being late for Mass.	
	I did not abstain or fast according to Church teaching (one hour before receiving Jesus in Eucharist, no meat on Friday during Lent, etc.).	
	I laughed or distracted others in church.	
✔	The Lord Says, "You shall love your neighbor as yourself,"	
	I did not give my parent, guardian, or teacher right-away obedience.	
	I was disrespectful to my parent, guardian, or teacher.	

"The confession of evil works is the first beginning of good works."—St. Augustine

I did not do my chores without grumbling or needing to be nagged.	
I spoke uncharitably to my parent, guardian, teacher, friend, sibling, etc.	
I lied.	
I took something that did not belong to me.	
I teased someone.	
I hurt someone.	
I did not treat my body, a temple of the Holy Spirit, with respect (ate too much, dressed immodestly, avoided exercise, etc.).	
I did not respect other's personal space.	
I said unkind words to or about someone else.	
I became envious of something someone else has or has achieved.	
I became angry or envious and did not handle my feelings in a positive way.	
I was prideful or boastful.	
I could have helped somebody and chose not to.	
I could have shared and chose not to.	
I could have been charitable and chose not to.	

- Say, "**I am sorry for these and all of my sins.**"
- Listen to the priest and pray an **Act of Contrition**:
  Act of Contrition - My God, I am sorry for my sins with all my heart. In choosing to do wrong and failing to do good, I have sinned against You whom I should love above all things. I firmly intend, with Your help, to do penance, to sin no more, and to avoid whatever leads me to sin. Our Savior Jesus Christ suffered and died for us. In His Name, my God, have mercy. Amen.
  Or
  Act of Contrition: O my God, I am heartily sorry for having offended You and I detest all my sins, because I dread the loss of heaven and the pains of hell. But most of all because I have offended You, my God, who are all good and deserving of all my love. I firmly resolve with the help of Your grace, to confess my sins, to do penance and to amend my life. Amen.

- Priest will say words of absolution (forgiveness). Make the Sign of the Cross.
- If he closes by saying, "Give thanks to the Lord for He is good," answer, "**For His mercy endures forever.**"
- Perform your penance.
- Thank God.

"The confession of evil works is the first beginning of good works."—St. Augustine

Today's Date: _____

Before Confession:

- Pray, "Come Holy Spirit" and make an Examination of Conscience. (Chapter 2)
- Pray for your confessor.

During Confession

- Priest welcomes you. Make the Sign of the Cross.
- Say "**Bless me Father, for I have sinned, this is my First Confession,**" or "**Bless me Father, for I have sinned, my last Confession was** _____ **(days, weeks, months) ago.**"
- Tell the priest your sins below:

✔	The Lord says, "You Shall Love the Lord Your God with your whole heart."	# Of Times?
	I did not obey God right away.	
	I doubted God's love for me.	
	I did not use all the graces God gave me to become closer to Him.	
	I did not pray my daily prayers (morning, evening, meals).	
	I put other things before God (friends, toys, games, and money).	
	I did not try to do my best for Jesus, even when I had to do things I didn't want to.	
	I spent money unwisely.	
	I placed my faith things other than God (good luck charms, etc.)	
	I said God's name in anger or frustration and / or spoke disrespectfully of God or Our Lady.	
	I used bad words (swear words).	
	I did not show reverence toward sacred persons, places, and things (e.g., the Pope, Bishop, priests, nuns, brothers, crucifixes, sacramentals, etc.).	
	I missed Mass on purpose on a Sunday or Holy Day of Obligation.	
	I was late for Mass or my behavior played a factor in our being late for Mass.	
	I did not abstain or fast according to Church teaching (one hour before receiving Jesus in Eucharist, no meat on Friday during Lent, etc.).	
	I laughed or distracted others in church.	
✔	The Lord Says, "You shall love your neighbor as yourself,"	
	I did not give my parent, guardian, or teacher right-away obedience.	
	I was disrespectful to my parent, guardian, or teacher.	

"The confession of evil works is the first beginning of good works."—St. Augustine

I did not do my chores without grumbling or needing to be nagged.	
I spoke uncharitably to my parent, guardian, teacher, friend, sibling, etc.	
I lied.	
I took something that did not belong to me.	
I teased someone.	
I hurt someone.	
I did not treat my body, a temple of the Holy Spirit, with respect (ate too much, dressed immodestly, avoided exercise, etc.).	
I did not respect other's personal space.	
I said unkind words to or about someone else.	
I became envious of something someone else has or has achieved.	
I became angry or envious and did not handle my feelings in a positive way.	
I was prideful or boastful.	
I could have helped somebody and chose not to.	
I could have shared and chose not to.	
I could have been charitable and chose not to.	

- Say, "**I am sorry for these and all of my sins.**"
- Listen to the priest and pray an **Act of Contrition**:
  Act of Contrition - My God, I am sorry for my sins with all my heart. In choosing to do wrong and failing to do good, I have sinned against You whom I should love above all things. I firmly intend, with Your help, to do penance, to sin no more, and to avoid whatever leads me to sin. Our Savior Jesus Christ suffered and died for us. In His Name, my God, have mercy. Amen.
  Or
  Act of Contrition: O my God, I am heartily sorry for having offended You and I detest all my sins, because I dread the loss of heaven and the pains of hell. But most of all because I have offended You, my God, who are all good and deserving of all my love. I firmly resolve with the help of Your grace, to confess my sins, to do penance and to amend my life. Amen.

- Priest will say words of absolution (forgiveness). Make the Sign of the Cross.
- If he closes by saying, "Give thanks to the Lord for He is good," answer, **"For His mercy endures forever."**
- Perform your penance.
- Thank God.

"The confession of evil works is the first beginning of good works."—St. Augustine

Today's Date: _____

Before Confession:

- Pray, "Come Holy Spirit" and make an Examination of Conscience. (Chapter 2)
- Pray for your confessor.

During Confession

- Priest welcomes you. Make the Sign of the Cross.
- Say "**Bless me Father, for I have sinned, this is my First Confession,**" or "**Bless me Father, for I have sinned, my last Confession was _____ (days, weeks, months) ago.**"
- Tell the priest your sins below:

✔	The Lord says, "You Shall Love the Lord Your God with your whole heart."	# Of Times?
	I did not obey God right away.	
	I doubted God's love for me.	
	I did not use all the graces God gave me to become closer to Him.	
	I did not pray my daily prayers (morning, evening, meals).	
	I put other things before God (friends, toys, games, and money).	
	I did not try to do my best for Jesus, even when I had to do things I didn't want to.	
	I spent money unwisely.	
	I placed my faith things other than God (good luck charms, etc.)	
	I said God's name in anger or frustration and / or spoke disrespectfully of God or Our Lady.	
	I used bad words (swear words).	
	I did not show reverence toward sacred persons, places, and things (e.g., the Pope, Bishop, priests, nuns, brothers, crucifixes, sacramentals, etc.).	
	I missed Mass on purpose on a Sunday or Holy Day of Obligation.	
	I was late for Mass or my behavior played a factor in our being late for Mass.	
	I did not abstain or fast according to Church teaching (one hour before receiving Jesus in Eucharist, no meat on Friday during Lent, etc.).	
	I laughed or distracted others in church.	
✔	The Lord Says, "You shall love your neighbor as yourself,"	
	I did not give my parent, guardian, or teacher right-away obedience.	
	I was disrespectful to my parent, guardian, or teacher.	

"The confession of evil works is the first beginning of good works."—St. Augustine

	I did not do my chores without grumbling or needing to be nagged.	
	I spoke uncharitably to my parent, guardian, teacher, friend, sibling, etc.	
	I lied.	
	I took something that did not belong to me.	
	I teased someone.	
	I hurt someone.	
	I did not treat my body, a temple of the Holy Spirit, with respect (ate too much, dressed immodestly, avoided exercise, etc.).	
	I did not respect other's personal space.	
	I said unkind words to or about someone else.	
	I became envious of something someone else has or has achieved.	
	I became angry or envious and did not handle my feelings in a positive way.	
	I was prideful or boastful.	
	I could have helped somebody and chose not to.	
	I could have shared and chose not to.	
	I could have been charitable and chose not to.	

- Say, "**I am sorry for these and all of my sins.**"
- Listen to the priest and pray an **Act of Contrition**:
  Act of Contrition - My God, I am sorry for my sins with all my heart. In choosing to do wrong and failing to do good, I have sinned against You whom I should love above all things. I firmly intend, with Your help, to do penance, to sin no more, and to avoid whatever leads me to sin. Our Savior Jesus Christ suffered and died for us. In His Name, my God, have mercy. Amen.
  Or
  Act of Contrition: O my God, I am heartily sorry for having offended You and I detest all my sins, because I dread the loss of heaven and the pains of hell. But most of all because I have offended You, my God, who are all good and deserving of all my love. I firmly resolve with the help of Your grace, to confess my sins, to do penance and to amend my life. Amen.

- Priest will say words of absolution (forgiveness). Make the Sign of the Cross.
- If he closes by saying, "Give thanks to the Lord for He is good," answer, **"For His mercy endures forever."**
- Perform your penance.
- Thank God.

"The confession of evil works is the first beginning of good works."—St. Augustine

Today's Date: _____

Before Confession:
- Pray, "Come Holy Spirit" and make an Examination of Conscience. (Chapter 2)
- Pray for your confessor.

During Confession
- Priest welcomes you. Make the Sign of the Cross.
- Say "**Bless me Father, for I have sinned, this is my First Confession,**" or "**Bless me Father, for I have sinned, my last Confession was _____ (days, weeks, months) ago.**"
- Tell the priest your sins below:

✔	The Lord says, "You Shall Love the Lord Your God with your whole heart."	# Of Times?
	I did not obey God right away.	
	I doubted God's love for me.	
	I did not use all the graces God gave me to become closer to Him.	
	I did not pray my daily prayers (morning, evening, meals).	
	I put other things before God (friends, toys, games, and money).	
	I did not try to do my best for Jesus, even when I had to do things I didn't want to.	
	I spent money unwisely.	
	I placed my faith things other than God (good luck charms, etc.)	
	I said God's name in anger or frustration and / or spoke disrespectfully of God or Our Lady.	
	I used bad words (swear words).	
	I did not show reverence toward sacred persons, places, and things (e.g., the Pope, Bishop, priests, nuns, brothers, crucifixes, sacramentals, etc.).	
	I missed Mass on purpose on a Sunday or Holy Day of Obligation.	
	I was late for Mass or my behavior played a factor in our being late for Mass.	
	I did not abstain or fast according to Church teaching (one hour before receiving Jesus in Eucharist, no meat on Friday during Lent, etc.).	
	I laughed or distracted others in church.	
✔	The Lord Says, "You shall love your neighbor as yourself."	
	I did not give my parent, guardian, or teacher right-away obedience.	
	I was disrespectful to my parent, guardian, or teacher.	

"The confession of evil works is the first beginning of good works."—St. Augustine

I did not do my chores without grumbling or needing to be nagged.	
I spoke uncharitably to my parent, guardian, teacher, friend, sibling, etc.	
I lied.	
I took something that did not belong to me.	
I teased someone.	
I hurt someone.	
I did not treat my body, a temple of the Holy Spirit, with respect (ate too much, dressed immodestly, avoided exercise, etc.).	
I did not respect other's personal space.	
I said unkind words to or about someone else.	
I became envious of something someone else has or has achieved.	
I became angry or envious and did not handle my feelings in a positive way.	
I was prideful or boastful.	
I could have helped somebody and chose not to.	
I could have shared and chose not to.	
I could have been charitable and chose not to.	

- Say, "**I am sorry for these and all of my sins.**"
- Listen to the priest and pray an **Act of Contrition**:
  Act of Contrition - My God, I am sorry for my sins with all my heart. In choosing to do wrong and failing to do good, I have sinned against You whom I should love above all things. I firmly intend, with Your help, to do penance, to sin no more, and to avoid whatever leads me to sin. Our Savior Jesus Christ suffered and died for us. In His Name, my God, have mercy. Amen.
  Or
  Act of Contrition: O my God, I am heartily sorry for having offended You and I detest all my sins, because I dread the loss of heaven and the pains of hell. But most of all because I have offended You, my God, who are all good and deserving of all my love. I firmly resolve with the help of Your grace, to confess my sins, to do penance and to amend my life. Amen.

- Priest will say words of absolution (forgiveness). Make the Sign of the Cross.
- If he closes by saying, "Give thanks to the Lord for He is good," answer, **"For His mercy endures forever."**
- Perform your penance.
- Thank God.

"The confession of evil works is the first beginning of good works."—St. Augustine

Today's Date: _____

Before Confession:

- Pray, "Come Holy Spirit" and make an Examination of Conscience. (Chapter 2)
- Pray for your confessor.

During Confession

- Priest welcomes you. Make the Sign of the Cross.
- Say "**Bless me Father, for I have sinned, this is my First Confession,**" or "**Bless me Father, for I have sinned, my last Confession was** _____ **(days, weeks, months) ago.**"
- Tell the priest your sins below:

✔	The Lord says, "You Shall Love the Lord Your God with your whole heart."	# Of Times?
	I did not obey God right away.	
	I doubted God's love for me.	
	I did not use all the graces God gave me to become closer to Him.	
	I did not pray my daily prayers (morning, evening, meals).	
	I put other things before God (friends, toys, games, and money).	
	I did not try to do my best for Jesus, even when I had to do things I didn't want to.	
	I spent money unwisely.	
	I placed my faith things other than God (good luck charms, etc.)	
	I said God's name in anger or frustration and / or spoke disrespectfully of God or Our Lady.	
	I used bad words (swear words).	
	I did not show reverence toward sacred persons, places, and things (e.g., the Pope, Bishop, priests, nuns, brothers, crucifixes, sacramentals, etc.).	
	I missed Mass on purpose on a Sunday or Holy Day of Obligation.	
	I was late for Mass or my behavior played a factor in our being late for Mass.	
	I did not abstain or fast according to Church teaching (one hour before receiving Jesus in Eucharist, no meat on Friday during Lent, etc.).	
	I laughed or distracted others in church.	
✔	The Lord Says, "You shall love your neighbor as yourself,"	
	I did not give my parent, guardian, or teacher right-away obedience.	
	I was disrespectful to my parent, guardian, or teacher.	

"The confession of evil works is the first beginning of good works."—St. Augustine

I did not do my chores without grumbling or needing to be nagged.	
I spoke uncharitably to my parent, guardian, teacher, friend, sibling, etc.	
I lied.	
I took something that did not belong to me.	
I teased someone.	
I hurt someone.	
I did not treat my body, a temple of the Holy Spirit, with respect (ate too much, dressed immodestly, avoided exercise, etc.).	
I did not respect other's personal space.	
I said unkind words to or about someone else.	
I became envious of something someone else has or has achieved.	
I became angry or envious and did not handle my feelings in a positive way.	
I was prideful or boastful.	
I could have helped somebody and chose not to.	
I could have shared and chose not to.	
I could have been charitable and chose not to.	

- Say, "**I am sorry for these and all of my sins.**"
- Listen to the priest and pray an **Act of Contrition**:

    Act of Contrition - My God, I am sorry for my sins with all my heart. In choosing to do wrong and failing to do good, I have sinned against You whom I should love above all things. I firmly intend, with Your help, to do penance, to sin no more, and to avoid whatever leads me to sin. Our Savior Jesus Christ suffered and died for us. In His Name, my God, have mercy. Amen.

    Or

    Act of Contrition: O my God, I am heartily sorry for having offended You and I detest all my sins, because I dread the loss of heaven and the pains of hell. But most of all because I have offended You, my God, who are all good and deserving of all my love. I firmly resolve with the help of Your grace, to confess my sins, to do penance and to amend my life. Amen.

- Priest will say words of absolution (forgiveness). Make the Sign of the Cross.
- If he closes by saying, "Give thanks to the Lord for He is good," answer, **"For His mercy endures forever."**
- Perform your penance.
- Thank God.

"The confession of evil works is the first beginning of good works."—St. Augustine

Today's Date: _____

Before Confession:

- Pray, "Come Holy Spirit" and make an Examination of Conscience. (Chapter 2)
- Pray for your confessor.

During Confession

- Priest welcomes you. Make the Sign of the Cross.
- Say "**Bless me Father, for I have sinned, this is my First Confession,**" or "**Bless me Father, for I have sinned, my last Confession was** _____ **(days, weeks, months) ago.**"
- Tell the priest your sins below:

✔ The Lord says, "You Shall Love the Lord Your God with your whole heart."	# Of Times?
I did not obey God right away.	
I doubted God's love for me.	
I did not use all the graces God gave me to become closer to Him.	
I did not pray my daily prayers (morning, evening, meals).	
I put other things before God (friends, toys, games, and money).	
I did not try to do my best for Jesus, even when I had to do things I didn't want to.	
I spent money unwisely.	
I placed my faith things other than God (good luck charms, etc.)	
I said God's name in anger or frustration and / or spoke disrespectfully of God or Our Lady.	
I used bad words (swear words).	
I did not show reverence toward sacred persons, places, and things (e.g., the Pope, Bishop, priests, nuns, brothers, crucifixes, sacramentals, etc.).	
I missed Mass on purpose on a Sunday or Holy Day of Obligation.	
I was late for Mass or my behavior played a factor in our being late for Mass.	
I did not abstain or fast according to Church teaching (one hour before receiving Jesus in Eucharist, no meat on Friday during Lent, etc.).	
I laughed or distracted others in church.	
✔ The Lord Says, "You shall love your neighbor as yourself,"	
I did not give my parent, guardian, or teacher right-away obedience.	
I was disrespectful to my parent, guardian, or teacher.	

"The confession of evil works is the first beginning of good works."—St. Augustine

	I did not do my chores without grumbling or needing to be nagged.	
	I spoke uncharitably to my parent, guardian, teacher, friend, sibling, etc.	
	I lied.	
	I took something that did not belong to me.	
	I teased someone.	
	I hurt someone.	
	I did not treat my body, a temple of the Holy Spirit, with respect (ate too much, dressed immodestly, avoided exercise, etc.).	
	I did not respect other's personal space.	
	I said unkind words to or about someone else.	
	I became envious of something someone else has or has achieved.	
	I became angry or envious and did not handle my feelings in a positive way.	
	I was prideful or boastful.	
	I could have helped somebody and chose not to.	
	I could have shared and chose not to.	
	I could have been charitable and chose not to.	

- Say, "**I am sorry for these and all of my sins.**"
- Listen to the priest and pray an **Act of Contrition**:
  Act of Contrition - My God, I am sorry for my sins with all my heart. In choosing to do wrong and failing to do good, I have sinned against You whom I should love above all things. I firmly intend, with Your help, to do penance, to sin no more, and to avoid whatever leads me to sin. Our Savior Jesus Christ suffered and died for us. In His Name, my God, have mercy. Amen.
  Or
  Act of Contrition: O my God, I am heartily sorry for having offended You and I detest all my sins, because I dread the loss of heaven and the pains of hell. But most of all because I have offended You, my God, who are all good and deserving of all my love. I firmly resolve with the help of Your grace, to confess my sins, to do penance and to amend my life. Amen.

- Priest will say words of absolution (forgiveness). Make the Sign of the Cross.
- If he closes by saying, "Give thanks to the Lord for He is good," answer, "**For His mercy endures forever.**"
- Perform your penance.
- Thank God.

"The confession of evil works is the first beginning of good works."—St. Augustine

Today's Date: _____

Before Confession:

- Pray, "Come Holy Spirit" and make an Examination of Conscience. (Chapter 2)
- Pray for your confessor.

During Confession

- Priest welcomes you. Make the Sign of the Cross.
- Say "**Bless me Father, for I have sinned, this is my First Confession,**" or "**Bless me Father, for I have sinned, my last Confession was _____ (days, weeks, months) ago.**"
- Tell the priest your sins below:

✔	The Lord says, "You Shall Love the Lord Your God with your whole heart."	# Of Times?
	I did not obey God right away.	
	I doubted God's love for me.	
	I did not use all the graces God gave me to become closer to Him.	
	I did not pray my daily prayers (morning, evening, meals).	
	I put other things before God (friends, toys, games, and money).	
	I did not try to do my best for Jesus, even when I had to do things I didn't want to.	
	I spent money unwisely.	
	I placed my faith things other than God (good luck charms, etc.)	
	I said God's name in anger or frustration and / or spoke disrespectfully of God or Our Lady.	
	I used bad words (swear words).	
	I did not show reverence toward sacred persons, places, and things (e.g., the Pope, Bishop, priests, nuns, brothers, crucifixes, sacramentals, etc.).	
	I missed Mass on purpose on a Sunday or Holy Day of Obligation.	
	I was late for Mass or my behavior played a factor in our being late for Mass.	
	I did not abstain or fast according to Church teaching (one hour before receiving Jesus in Eucharist, no meat on Friday during Lent, etc.).	
	I laughed or distracted others in church.	
✔	The Lord Says, "You shall love your neighbor as yourself,"	
	I did not give my parent, guardian, or teacher right-away obedience.	
	I was disrespectful to my parent, guardian, or teacher.	

"The confession of evil works is the first beginning of good works."—St. Augustine

I did not do my chores without grumbling or needing to be nagged.	
I spoke uncharitably to my parent, guardian, teacher, friend, sibling, etc.	
I lied.	
I took something that did not belong to me.	
I teased someone.	
I hurt someone.	
I did not treat my body, a temple of the Holy Spirit, with respect (ate too much, dressed immodestly, avoided exercise, etc.).	
I did not respect other's personal space.	
I said unkind words to or about someone else.	
I became envious of something someone else has or has achieved.	
I became angry or envious and did not handle my feelings in a positive way.	
I was prideful or boastful.	
I could have helped somebody and chose not to.	
I could have shared and chose not to.	
I could have been charitable and chose not to.	

- Say, "**I am sorry for these and all of my sins.**"
- Listen to the priest and pray an **Act of Contrition**:
  Act of Contrition - My God, I am sorry for my sins with all my heart. In choosing to do wrong and failing to do good, I have sinned against You whom I should love above all things. I firmly intend, with Your help, to do penance, to sin no more, and to avoid whatever leads me to sin. Our Savior Jesus Christ suffered and died for us. In His Name, my God, have mercy. Amen.
  Or
  Act of Contrition: O my God, I am heartily sorry for having offended You and I detest all my sins, because I dread the loss of heaven and the pains of hell. But most of all because I have offended You, my God, who are all good and deserving of all my love. I firmly resolve with the help of Your grace, to confess my sins, to do penance and to amend my life. Amen.

- Priest will say words of absolution (forgiveness). Make the Sign of the Cross.
- If he closes by saying, "Give thanks to the Lord for He is good," answer, **"For His mercy endures forever."**
- Perform your penance.
- Thank God.

"The confession of evil works is the first beginning of good works."—St. Augustine

Today's Date: _____

Before Confession:
- Pray, "Come Holy Spirit" and make an Examination of Conscience. (Chapter 2)
- Pray for your confessor.

During Confession
- Priest welcomes you. Make the Sign of the Cross.
- Say "**Bless me Father, for I have sinned, this is my First Confession,**" or "**Bless me Father, for I have sinned, my last Confession was _____ (days, weeks, months) ago.**"
- Tell the priest your sins below:

✔	The Lord says, "You Shall Love the Lord Your God with your whole heart."	# Of Times?
	I did not obey God right away.	
	I doubted God's love for me.	
	I did not use all the graces God gave me to become closer to Him.	
	I did not pray my daily prayers (morning, evening, meals).	
	I put other things before God (friends, toys, games, and money).	
	I did not try to do my best for Jesus, even when I had to do things I didn't want to.	
	I spent money unwisely.	
	I placed my faith things other than God (good luck charms, etc.)	
	I said God's name in anger or frustration and / or spoke disrespectfully of God or Our Lady.	
	I used bad words (swear words).	
	I did not show reverence toward sacred persons, places, and things (e.g., the Pope, Bishop, priests, nuns, brothers, crucifixes, sacramentals, etc.).	
	I missed Mass on purpose on a Sunday or Holy Day of Obligation.	
	I was late for Mass or my behavior played a factor in our being late for Mass.	
	I did not abstain or fast according to Church teaching (one hour before receiving Jesus in Eucharist, no meat on Friday during Lent, etc.).	
	I laughed or distracted others in church.	
✔	The Lord Says, "You shall love your neighbor as yourself,"	
	I did not give my parent, guardian, or teacher right-away obedience.	
	I was disrespectful to my parent, guardian, or teacher.	

"The confession of evil works is the first beginning of good works."—*St. Augustine*

I did not do my chores without grumbling or needing to be nagged.	
I spoke uncharitably to my parent, guardian, teacher, friend, sibling, etc.	
I lied.	
I took something that did not belong to me.	
I teased someone.	
I hurt someone.	
I did not treat my body, a temple of the Holy Spirit, with respect (ate too much, dressed immodestly, avoided exercise, etc.).	
I did not respect other's personal space.	
I said unkind words to or about someone else.	
I became envious of something someone else has or has achieved.	
I became angry or envious and did not handle my feelings in a positive way.	
I was prideful or boastful.	
I could have helped somebody and chose not to.	
I could have shared and chose not to.	
I could have been charitable and chose not to.	

- Say, "**I am sorry for these and all of my sins.**"
- Listen to the priest and pray an **Act of Contrition**:
  Act of Contrition - My God, I am sorry for my sins with all my heart. In choosing to do wrong and failing to do good, I have sinned against You whom I should love above all things. I firmly intend, with Your help, to do penance, to sin no more, and to avoid whatever leads me to sin. Our Savior Jesus Christ suffered and died for us. In His Name, my God, have mercy. Amen.
  Or
  Act of Contrition: O my God, I am heartily sorry for having offended You and I detest all my sins, because I dread the loss of heaven and the pains of hell. But most of all because I have offended You, my God, who are all good and deserving of all my love. I firmly resolve with the help of Your grace, to confess my sins, to do penance and to amend my life. Amen.

- Priest will say words of absolution (forgiveness). Make the Sign of the Cross.
- If he closes by saying, "Give thanks to the Lord for He is good," answer, **"For His mercy endures forever."**
- Perform your penance.
- Thank God.

"The confession of evil works is the first beginning of good works."—St. Augustine

Today's Date: _____

Before Confession:

- Pray, "Come Holy Spirit" and make an Examination of Conscience. (Chapter 2)
- Pray for your confessor.

During Confession

- Priest welcomes you. Make the Sign of the Cross.
- Say "**Bless me Father, for I have sinned, this is my First Confession,**" or "**Bless me Father, for I have sinned, my last Confession was** _____ **(days, weeks, months) ago.**"
- Tell the priest your sins below:

✔ The Lord says, "You Shall Love the Lord Your God with your whole heart."	# Of Times?
I did not obey God right away.	
I doubted God's love for me.	
I did not use all the graces God gave me to become closer to Him.	
I did not pray my daily prayers (morning, evening, meals).	
I put other things before God (friends, toys, games, and money).	
I did not try to do my best for Jesus, even when I had to do things I didn't want to.	
I spent money unwisely.	
I placed my faith things other than God (good luck charms, etc.)	
I said God's name in anger or frustration and / or spoke disrespectfully of God or Our Lady.	
I used bad words (swear words).	
I did not show reverence toward sacred persons, places, and things (e.g., the Pope, Bishop, priests, nuns, brothers, crucifixes, sacramentals, etc.).	
I missed Mass on purpose on a Sunday or Holy Day of Obligation.	
I was late for Mass or my behavior played a factor in our being late for Mass.	
I did not abstain or fast according to Church teaching (one hour before receiving Jesus in Eucharist, no meat on Friday during Lent, etc.).	
I laughed or distracted others in church.	
✔ The Lord Says, "You shall love your neighbor as yourself,"	
I did not give my parent, guardian, or teacher right-away obedience.	
I was disrespectful to my parent, guardian, or teacher.	

"The confession of evil works is the first beginning of good works."—St. Augustine

I did not do my chores without grumbling or needing to be nagged.	
I spoke uncharitably to my parent, guardian, teacher, friend, sibling, etc.	
I lied.	
I took something that did not belong to me.	
I teased someone.	
I hurt someone.	
I did not treat my body, a temple of the Holy Spirit, with respect (ate too much, dressed immodestly, avoided exercise, etc.).	
I did not respect other's personal space.	
I said unkind words to or about someone else.	
I became envious of something someone else has or has achieved.	
I became angry or envious and did not handle my feelings in a positive way.	
I was prideful or boastful.	
I could have helped somebody and chose not to.	
I could have shared and chose not to.	
I could have been charitable and chose not to.	

- Say, "**I am sorry for these and all of my sins.**"
- Listen to the priest and pray an **Act of Contrition**:
  Act of Contrition - My God, I am sorry for my sins with all my heart. In choosing to do wrong and failing to do good, I have sinned against You whom I should love above all things. I firmly intend, with Your help, to do penance, to sin no more, and to avoid whatever leads me to sin. Our Savior Jesus Christ suffered and died for us. In His Name, my God, have mercy. Amen.
  Or
  Act of Contrition: O my God, I am heartily sorry for having offended You and I detest all my sins, because I dread the loss of heaven and the pains of hell. But most of all because I have offended You, my God, who are all good and deserving of all my love. I firmly resolve with the help of Your grace, to confess my sins, to do penance and to amend my life. Amen.

- Priest will say words of absolution (forgiveness). Make the Sign of the Cross.
- If he closes by saying, "Give thanks to the Lord for He is good," answer, **"For His mercy endures forever."**
- Perform your penance.
- Thank God.

"The confession of evil works is the first beginning of good works."—*St. Augustine*

Today's Date: _____

Before Confession:

- Pray, "Come Holy Spirit" and make an Examination of Conscience. (Chapter 2)
- Pray for your confessor.

During Confession

- Priest welcomes you. Make the Sign of the Cross.
- Say "**Bless me Father, for I have sinned, this is my First Confession,**" or "**Bless me Father, for I have sinned, my last Confession was _____ (days, weeks, months) ago.**"
- Tell the priest your sins below:

✔	The Lord says, "You Shall Love the Lord Your God with your whole heart."	# Of Times?
	I did not obey God right away.	
	I doubted God's love for me.	
	I did not use all the graces God gave me to become closer to Him.	
	I did not pray my daily prayers (morning, evening, meals).	
	I put other things before God (friends, toys, games, and money).	
	I did not try to do my best for Jesus, even when I had to do things I didn't want to.	
	I spent money unwisely.	
	I placed my faith things other than God (good luck charms, etc.)	
	I said God's name in anger or frustration and / or spoke disrespectfully of God or Our Lady.	
	I used bad words (swear words).	
	I did not show reverence toward sacred persons, places, and things (e.g., the Pope, Bishop, priests, nuns, brothers, crucifixes, sacramentals, etc.).	
	I missed Mass on purpose on a Sunday or Holy Day of Obligation.	
	I was late for Mass or my behavior played a factor in our being late for Mass.	
	I did not abstain or fast according to Church teaching (one hour before receiving Jesus in Eucharist, no meat on Friday during Lent, etc.).	
	I laughed or distracted others in church.	
✔	The Lord Says, "You shall love your neighbor as yourself,"	
	I did not give my parent, guardian, or teacher right-away obedience.	
	I was disrespectful to my parent, guardian, or teacher.	

"The confession of evil works is the first beginning of good works."—St. Augustine

I did not do my chores without grumbling or needing to be nagged.	
I spoke uncharitably to my parent, guardian, teacher, friend, sibling, etc.	
I lied.	
I took something that did not belong to me.	
I teased someone.	
I hurt someone.	
I did not treat my body, a temple of the Holy Spirit, with respect (ate too much, dressed immodestly, avoided exercise, etc.).	
I did not respect other's personal space.	
I said unkind words to or about someone else.	
I became envious of something someone else has or has achieved.	
I became angry or envious and did not handle my feelings in a positive way.	
I was prideful or boastful.	
I could have helped somebody and chose not to.	
I could have shared and chose not to.	
I could have been charitable and chose not to.	

- Say, "**I am sorry for these and all of my sins.**"
- Listen to the priest and pray an **Act of Contrition**:

  Act of Contrition - My God, I am sorry for my sins with all my heart. In choosing to do wrong and failing to do good, I have sinned against You whom I should love above all things. I firmly intend, with Your help, to do penance, to sin no more, and to avoid whatever leads me to sin. Our Savior Jesus Christ suffered and died for us. In His Name, my God, have mercy. Amen.

  Or

  Act of Contrition: O my God, I am heartily sorry for having offended You and I detest all my sins, because I dread the loss of heaven and the pains of hell. But most of all because I have offended You, my God, who are all good and deserving of all my love. I firmly resolve with the help of Your grace, to confess my sins, to do penance and to amend my life. Amen.

- Priest will say words of absolution (forgiveness). Make the Sign of the Cross.
- If he closes by saying, "Give thanks to the Lord for He is good," answer, **"For His mercy endures forever."**
- Perform your penance.
- Thank God.

"The confession of evil works is the first beginning of good works."—St. Augustine

Today's Date: _____

Before Confession:

- Pray, "Come Holy Spirit" and make an Examination of Conscience. (Chapter 2)
- Pray for your confessor.

During Confession

- Priest welcomes you. Make the Sign of the Cross.
- Say "**Bless me Father, for I have sinned, this is my First Confession,**" or "**Bless me Father, for I have sinned, my last Confession was _____ (days, weeks, months) ago.**"
- Tell the priest your sins below:

✔	The Lord says, "You Shall Love the Lord Your God with your whole heart."	# Of Times?
	I did not obey God right away.	
	I doubted God's love for me.	
	I did not use all the graces God gave me to become closer to Him.	
	I did not pray my daily prayers (morning, evening, meals).	
	I put other things before God (friends, toys, games, and money).	
	I did not try to do my best for Jesus, even when I had to do things I didn't want to.	
	I spent money unwisely.	
	I placed my faith things other than God (good luck charms, etc.)	
	I said God's name in anger or frustration and / or spoke disrespectfully of God or Our Lady.	
	I used bad words (swear words).	
	I did not show reverence toward sacred persons, places, and things (e.g., the Pope, Bishop, priests, nuns, brothers, crucifixes, sacramentals, etc.).	
	I missed Mass on purpose on a Sunday or Holy Day of Obligation.	
	I was late for Mass or my behavior played a factor in our being late for Mass.	
	I did not abstain or fast according to Church teaching (one hour before receiving Jesus in Eucharist, no meat on Friday during Lent, etc.).	
	I laughed or distracted others in church.	
✔	The Lord Says, "You shall love your neighbor as yourself,"	
	I did not give my parent, guardian, or teacher right-away obedience.	
	I was disrespectful to my parent, guardian, or teacher.	

"The confession of evil works is the first beginning of good works."—*St. Augustine*

I did not do my chores without grumbling or needing to be nagged.	
I spoke uncharitably to my parent, guardian, teacher, friend, sibling, etc.	
I lied.	
I took something that did not belong to me.	
I teased someone.	
I hurt someone.	
I did not treat my body, a temple of the Holy Spirit, with respect (ate too much, dressed immodestly, avoided exercise, etc.).	
I did not respect other's personal space.	
I said unkind words to or about someone else.	
I became envious of something someone else has or has achieved.	
I became angry or envious and did not handle my feelings in a positive way.	
I was prideful or boastful.	
I could have helped somebody and chose not to.	
I could have shared and chose not to.	
I could have been charitable and chose not to.	

- Say, "**I am sorry for these and all of my sins.**"
- Listen to the priest and pray an **Act of Contrition**:
  Act of Contrition - My God, I am sorry for my sins with all my heart. In choosing to do wrong and failing to do good, I have sinned against You whom I should love above all things. I firmly intend, with Your help, to do penance, to sin no more, and to avoid whatever leads me to sin. Our Savior Jesus Christ suffered and died for us. In His Name, my God, have mercy. Amen.
  Or
  Act of Contrition: O my God, I am heartily sorry for having offended You and I detest all my sins, because I dread the loss of heaven and the pains of hell. But most of all because I have offended You, my God, who are all good and deserving of all my love. I firmly resolve with the help of Your grace, to confess my sins, to do penance and to amend my life. Amen.

- Priest will say words of absolution (forgiveness). Make the Sign of the Cross.
- If he closes by saying, "Give thanks to the Lord for He is good," answer, **"For His mercy endures forever."**
- Perform your penance.
- Thank God.

"The confession of evil works is the first beginning of good works."—St. Augustine

Today's Date: _____

Before Confession:
- Pray, "Come Holy Spirit" and make an Examination of Conscience. (Chapter 2)
- Pray for your confessor.

During Confession
- Priest welcomes you. Make the Sign of the Cross.
- Say "**Bless me Father, for I have sinned, this is my First Confession,**" or "**Bless me Father, for I have sinned, my last Confession was _____ (days, weeks, months) ago.**"
- Tell the priest your sins below:

✔ The Lord says, "You Shall Love the Lord Your God with your whole heart."	# Of Times?
I did not obey God right away.	
I doubted God's love for me.	
I did not use all the graces God gave me to become closer to Him.	
I did not pray my daily prayers (morning, evening, meals).	
I put other things before God (friends, toys, games, and money).	
I did not try to do my best for Jesus, even when I had to do things I didn't want to.	
I spent money unwisely.	
I placed my faith things other than God (good luck charms, etc.)	
I said God's name in anger or frustration and / or spoke disrespectfully of God or Our Lady.	
I used bad words (swear words).	
I did not show reverence toward sacred persons, places, and things (e.g., the Pope, Bishop, priests, nuns, brothers, crucifixes, sacramentals, etc.).	
I missed Mass on purpose on a Sunday or Holy Day of Obligation.	
I was late for Mass or my behavior played a factor in our being late for Mass.	
I did not abstain or fast according to Church teaching (one hour before receiving Jesus in Eucharist, no meat on Friday during Lent, etc.).	
I laughed or distracted others in church.	
✔ The Lord Says, "You shall love your neighbor as yourself,"	
I did not give my parent, guardian, or teacher right-away obedience.	
I was disrespectful to my parent, guardian, or teacher.	

"The confession of evil works is the first beginning of good works."—St. Augustine

I did not do my chores without grumbling or needing to be nagged.	
I spoke uncharitably to my parent, guardian, teacher, friend, sibling, etc.	
I lied.	
I took something that did not belong to me.	
I teased someone.	
I hurt someone.	
I did not treat my body, a temple of the Holy Spirit, with respect (ate too much, dressed immodestly, avoided exercise, etc.).	
I did not respect other's personal space.	
I said unkind words to or about someone else.	
I became envious of something someone else has or has achieved.	
I became angry or envious and did not handle my feelings in a positive way.	
I was prideful or boastful.	
I could have helped somebody and chose not to.	
I could have shared and chose not to.	
I could have been charitable and chose not to.	

- Say, "**I am sorry for these and all of my sins.**"
- Listen to the priest and pray an **Act of Contrition**:
  Act of Contrition - My God, I am sorry for my sins with all my heart. In choosing to do wrong and failing to do good, I have sinned against You whom I should love above all things. I firmly intend, with Your help, to do penance, to sin no more, and to avoid whatever leads me to sin. Our Savior Jesus Christ suffered and died for us. In His Name, my God, have mercy. Amen.
  Or
  Act of Contrition: O my God, I am heartily sorry for having offended You and I detest all my sins, because I dread the loss of heaven and the pains of hell. But most of all because I have offended You, my God, who are all good and deserving of all my love. I firmly resolve with the help of Your grace, to confess my sins, to do penance and to amend my life. Amen.

- Priest will say words of absolution (forgiveness). Make the Sign of the Cross.
- If he closes by saying, "Give thanks to the Lord for He is good," answer, "**For His mercy endures forever.**"
- Perform your penance.
- Thank God.

"The confession of evil works is the first beginning of good works."—St. Augustine

Today's Date: _____

Before Confession:

- Pray, "Come Holy Spirit" and make an Examination of Conscience. (Chapter 2)
- Pray for your confessor.

During Confession

- Priest welcomes you. Make the Sign of the Cross.
- Say "**Bless me Father, for I have sinned, this is my First Confession,**" or "**Bless me Father, for I have sinned, my last Confession was** _____ (**days, weeks, months**) **ago.**"
- Tell the priest your sins below:

✔	The Lord says, "You Shall Love the Lord Your God with your whole heart."	# Of Times?
	I did not obey God right away.	
	I doubted God's love for me.	
	I did not use all the graces God gave me to become closer to Him.	
	I did not pray my daily prayers (morning, evening, meals).	
	I put other things before God (friends, toys, games, and money).	
	I did not try to do my best for Jesus, even when I had to do things I didn't want to.	
	I spent money unwisely.	
	I placed my faith things other than God (good luck charms, etc.)	
	I said God's name in anger or frustration and / or spoke disrespectfully of God or Our Lady.	
	I used bad words (swear words).	
	I did not show reverence toward sacred persons, places, and things (e.g., the Pope, Bishop, priests, nuns, brothers, crucifixes, sacramentals, etc.).	
	I missed Mass on purpose on a Sunday or Holy Day of Obligation.	
	I was late for Mass or my behavior played a factor in our being late for Mass.	
	I did not abstain or fast according to Church teaching (one hour before receiving Jesus in Eucharist, no meat on Friday during Lent, etc.).	
	I laughed or distracted others in church.	
✔	The Lord Says, "You shall love your neighbor as yourself."	
	I did not give my parent, guardian, or teacher right-away obedience.	
	I was disrespectful to my parent, guardian, or teacher.	

"The confession of evil works is the first beginning of good works."—*St. Augustine*

I did not do my chores without grumbling or needing to be nagged.	
I spoke uncharitably to my parent, guardian, teacher, friend, sibling, etc.	
I lied.	
I took something that did not belong to me.	
I teased someone.	
I hurt someone.	
I did not treat my body, a temple of the Holy Spirit, with respect (ate too much, dressed immodestly, avoided exercise, etc.).	
I did not respect other's personal space.	
I said unkind words to or about someone else.	
I became envious of something someone else has or has achieved.	
I became angry or envious and did not handle my feelings in a positive way.	
I was prideful or boastful.	
I could have helped somebody and chose not to.	
I could have shared and chose not to.	
I could have been charitable and chose not to.	

- Say, "**I am sorry for these and all of my sins.**"
- Listen to the priest and pray an **Act of Contrition**:

    Act of Contrition - My God, I am sorry for my sins with all my heart. In choosing to do wrong and failing to do good, I have sinned against You whom I should love above all things. I firmly intend, with Your help, to do penance, to sin no more, and to avoid whatever leads me to sin. Our Savior Jesus Christ suffered and died for us. In His Name, my God, have mercy. Amen.

    Or

    Act of Contrition: O my God, I am heartily sorry for having offended You and I detest all my sins, because I dread the loss of heaven and the pains of hell. But most of all because I have offended You, my God, who are all good and deserving of all my love. I firmly resolve with the help of Your grace, to confess my sins, to do penance and to amend my life. Amen.

- Priest will say words of absolution (forgiveness). Make the Sign of the Cross.
- If he closes by saying, "Give thanks to the Lord for He is good," answer, "**For His mercy endures forever.**"
- Perform your penance.
- Thank God.

"The confession of evil works is the first beginning of good works."—St. Augustine

Today's Date: _____

Before Confession:

- Pray, "Come Holy Spirit" and make an Examination of Conscience. (Chapter 2)
- Pray for your confessor.

During Confession

- Priest welcomes you. Make the Sign of the Cross.
- Say **"Bless me Father, for I have sinned, this is my First Confession,"** or **"Bless me Father, for I have sinned, my last Confession was** _____ **(days, weeks, months) ago."**
- Tell the priest your sins below:

✔	The Lord says, "You Shall Love the Lord Your God with your whole heart."	# Of Times?
	I did not obey God right away.	
	I doubted God's love for me.	
	I did not use all the graces God gave me to become closer to Him.	
	I did not pray my daily prayers (morning, evening, meals).	
	I put other things before God (friends, toys, games, and money).	
	I did not try to do my best for Jesus, even when I had to do things I didn't want to.	
	I spent money unwisely.	
	I placed my faith things other than God (good luck charms, etc.)	
	I said God's name in anger or frustration and / or spoke disrespectfully of God or Our Lady.	
	I used bad words (swear words).	
	I did not show reverence toward sacred persons, places, and things (e.g., the Pope, Bishop, priests, nuns, brothers, crucifixes, sacramentals, etc.).	
	I missed Mass on purpose on a Sunday or Holy Day of Obligation.	
	I was late for Mass or my behavior played a factor in our being late for Mass.	
	I did not abstain or fast according to Church teaching (one hour before receiving Jesus in Eucharist, no meat on Friday during Lent, etc.).	
	I laughed or distracted others in church.	
✔	The Lord Says, "You shall love your neighbor as yourself,"	
	I did not give my parent, guardian, or teacher right-away obedience.	
	I was disrespectful to my parent, guardian, or teacher.	

"The confession of evil works is the first beginning of good works."—St. Augustine

I did not do my chores without grumbling or needing to be nagged.	
I spoke uncharitably to my parent, guardian, teacher, friend, sibling, etc.	
I lied.	
I took something that did not belong to me.	
I teased someone.	
I hurt someone.	
I did not treat my body, a temple of the Holy Spirit, with respect (ate too much, dressed immodestly, avoided exercise, etc.).	
I did not respect other's personal space.	
I said unkind words to or about someone else.	
I became envious of something someone else has or has achieved.	
I became angry or envious and did not handle my feelings in a positive way.	
I was prideful or boastful.	
I could have helped somebody and chose not to.	
I could have shared and chose not to.	
I could have been charitable and chose not to.	

- Say, "**I am sorry for these and all of my sins.**"
- Listen to the priest and pray an **Act of Contrition**:
  Act of Contrition - My God, I am sorry for my sins with all my heart. In choosing to do wrong and failing to do good, I have sinned against You whom I should love above all things. I firmly intend, with Your help, to do penance, to sin no more, and to avoid whatever leads me to sin. Our Savior Jesus Christ suffered and died for us. In His Name, my God, have mercy. Amen.
  Or
  Act of Contrition: O my God, I am heartily sorry for having offended You and I detest all my sins, because I dread the loss of heaven and the pains of hell. But most of all because I have offended You, my God, who are all good and deserving of all my love. I firmly resolve with the help of Your grace, to confess my sins, to do penance and to amend my life. Amen.

- Priest will say words of absolution (forgiveness). Make the Sign of the Cross.
- If he closes by saying, "Give thanks to the Lord for He is good," answer, "**For His mercy endures forever.**"
- Perform your penance.
- Thank God.

"The confession of evil works is the first beginning of good works."—*St. Augustine*

CHAPTER 5

My Daily Examen - for Parent and Child

Part of the rich tradition of the Catholic Church is recognizing the need to reflect on the day's activities— to see how God worked in your life and how you responded to His grace. Saint Ignatius of Loyola developed a simple method by which you can review each day in a way that will help you grow in self-knowledge and help to follow God's Will. It can also help to prepare you to receive the Sacrament of Reconciliation. This practice is often called the Daily Examen. [4]

Practicing the Daily Examen as a family, but only with respect to sins that disrupt the happiness of family life, will foster a habit in your children when they are young, so that they may perform this on their own in the future. In making a Daily Examen, you will review your actions each day, which can carry over to "My Confession Worksheet." A simple way to employ this is by adding it to your evening prayer time, typically before the children go to bed, using following the five steps below.

Step 1

Place yourself in the presence of God
Ask the Holy Spirit to show you how to love Him more. Close your eyes for a minute or so and listen.

---

[4] Loyola Press, IgnatianSpirituality.com

Step 2

Review the day with gratitude
Think of at least one thing you are grateful for.

Step 3

Daily Review / Reflection
Talk about where you saw God in your day. Did He answer a prayer? Did He speak to you through a friend, book, movie, scripture, etc.?

Step 4

Virtues, Faults & Forgiveness
Work together to determine what fault each family member is struggling with and the virtue that opposes it (see below for a virtue vs. fault grid). Only tackle one fault at a time and ask God for the wisdom to discern which fault He would like each of you to address first. Restrict the discussion to faults that destroy a happy family life.

How are you doing? This is an opportunity to help one another daily to grow in virtue. Did you hurt anybody in word or action and not seek forgiveness from them? You may ask for and receive forgiveness from family members at this time.

It is important to note, however, that sins, by their very nature, are private (between each person and God, either directly or through the Sacrament of Reconciliation) and do **not** need to be revealed to other family members at this time. This is simply an opportunity for each family member to share their successes and failures in their attempt to grow in virtue each day within their level of comfort. No pressure should be placed upon family members to share their sins.

Step 5

Look toward tomorrow with hope
Ask God to help you tomorrow and promise to allow Him to lovingly guide you. [5]

---

[5] Loyola Press, IgnatianSpirituality.com

"The confession of evil works is the first beginning of good works."—*St. Augustine*

Below is an overview of the virtue and character traits along with their opposing faults and sins, to aid in your Daily Examen.

Virtue	Opposing Fault
Temperance – self-control	Gluttony – over indulgence
Charity – giving	Greed – avarice
Diligence – zeal for work	Sloth – laziness
Chastity – purity	Impurity
Forgiveness	Wrath – losing your temper, rage
Kindness – admiration	Envy – jealousy
Humility – humbleness	Pride – vanity
Patience	Impatience – quick tempered
Hope	Despair – no hope
Gentleness	Severity – cruelty
Obedience	Disobedience

"By prayerfully reviewing your day, you will experience the difference it can make in the way you live. If you make a habit of practicing the Daily Examen, you will grow closer to God in your thoughts and deeds and will be free to choose to follow him."[6]

---

[6] Loyola Press, IgnatianSpirituality.com

"The confession of evil works is the first beginning of good works."—St. Augustine

CHAPTER 6

Child's Prayer of Surrender and Commitment

Typically, both reception of the Sacrament of Reconciliation and First Holy Communion fall in the same year. A beautiful way of surrendering your life to Jesus, is to do this formally. Making a commitment, on your own volition, is empowering, and is made simple by using the following commitment card.

> *Dear Lord Jesus,*
> *Please come into my heart, and be the Lord of my life.*
> *Be my God and my Savior.*
> *Please send me Your Holy Spirit to make me your disciple.*
> *Thank you for giving up your life for me.*
> *Now I give my life to You.*
>
> Signed: _____
>
> Date: _____

In our home, we print the form on nice card stock and frame it for our children to display in their bedrooms. With your parent's help you can print a copy of this commitment card at: www. MyConfessionCompanion.com

CHAPTER 7

Traditional Catholic Prayers

Sign of the Cross
In the Name of the Father, and of the Son,
and of the Holy Spirit, Amen.

Our Father
Our Father, Who art in Heaven, hallowed be Thy
Name. Thy Kingdom come, Thy Will be done,
on earth, as it is in Heaven. Give us this day our daily
bread and forgive us our trespasses as we
forgive those who trespass against us; and lead us not
into temptation, but deliver us from evil. Amen.

Hail Mary
Hail Mary full of Grace, the Lord is with thee. Blessed are thou among
women and blessed is the fruit of thy womb, Jesus. Holy Mary Mother
of God, pray for us sinners now and at the hour of our death. Amen.

Glory Be
Glory be to the Father, and to the Son, and to the Holy Spirit, as it was
in the beginning, is now, and ever shall be, world without end. Amen.

Act of Faith

O MY GOD, I firmly believe that Thou art one God in Three Divine Persons, Father, Son and Holy Spirit. I believe that Thy Divine Son became Man, and died for our sins, and that He will come to judge the living and the dead. I believe these and all the truths which the Holy Catholic Church teaches, because Thou hast revealed them, Who canst neither deceive nor be deceived. Amen.

Act of Hope

O MY GOD, relying on Thy almighty power
and infinite mercy and promises, I
hope to obtain pardon of my sins, the help of Thy
grace, and Life Everlasting, through the merits of
Jesus Christ, my Lord and Redeemer. Amen.

Come Holy Spirit

Come Holy Spirit, fill the hearts of your faithful and kindle them in the fire of your love. Send forth Your Spirit and they shall be created. And You shall renew the face of the earth. Amen.

An Act of Love

Jesus, Mary, I love You! Save souls!

Act of Love

O MY GOD, I love Thee above all things, with my whole heart and soul, because Thou art all-good and worthy of all my love. I love my neighbor as myself for the love of Thee. I forgive all who have injured me, and ask pardon of all whom I have injured. Amen.

"The confession of evil works is the first beginning of good works."—St. Augustine

Act of Contrition

O my God, I am heartily sorry for having offended You and I detest all my sins, because I dread the loss of heaven and the pains of hell. But most of all because I have offended You, my God, who are all good and deserving of all my love. I firmly resolve with the help of Your grace, to confess my sins, to do penance and to amend my life. Amen.

Act of Contrition

My God, I am sorry for my sins with all my heart. In choosing to do wrong and failing to do good, I have sinned against you whom I should love above all things. I firmly intend, with your help, to do penance, to sin no more, and to avoid whatever leads me to sin. Our Savior Jesus Christ suffered and died for us. In His name, my God, have mercy. Amen.

Spiritual Communion

My Jesus, I believe that you are present in the most Blessed Sacrament.
I love You above all things and I desire to receive You into my soul.
Since I cannot now receive You sacramentally,
come at least spiritually into my heart.
I embrace You as if You have already come,
and unite myself wholly to You.
Never permit me to be separated from You. Amen.

Morning Offering

O Jesus, through the Immaculate Heart of Mary,
I offer You my prayers, works, joys and sufferings
of this day for all the intentions of Your Sacred Heart,
in union with the Holy Sacrifice of the Mass
throughout the world, in reparation for my sins,

"The confession of evil works is the first beginning of good works."—St. Augustine

for the intentions of all my relatives and friends,
and in particular for the intentions of the Holy Father. Amen

Guardian Angel Prayer
O Angel of God, my guardian dear, to whom God's love
commits me here; ever this day, be at my side,
to light, to guard, to rule and guide. Amen.

Prayer to Saint Michael the archangel
St. Michael the Archangel, defend us in battle.
Be our Protection against the wickedness and snares of the Devil.
May God rebuke him, we humbly pray, and do
thou, O Prince of the heavenly hosts,
by the power of God, thrust into hell Satan, and all the evil spirits,
who wander about the world seeking the ruin of souls. Amen.

Memorare
Remember, O most gracious Virgin Mary, that never was
it known that anyone who fled to thy protection, implored
thy help, or sought thy intercession was left unaided.
Inspired by this confidence, I fly unto thee, O Virgin of virgins,
my mother; to thee do I come, before thee I stand, sinful and
sorrowful. O Mother of the Word Incarnate, despise not my
petitions, but in thy mercy hear and answer me. Amen.

The Magnificat
My soul proclaims the greatness of the Lord,
my spirit rejoices in God my Savior for He has
looked with favor on His lowly servant.

"The confession of evil works is the first beginning of good works."—St. Augustine

From this day all generations will call me blessed: for
the Almighty has done great things for me,
and holy is His Name.

He has shown mercy for those who fear Him in every generation.
He has shown the strength of his arm, He has
scattered the proud in their conceit.

He has cast down the mighty from their
thrones, and has lifted up the lowly.
He has filled the hungry with good things,
and the rich He has sent empty away.

He has come to the help of His servant Israel for
He remembered His promise of mercy,
the promise He made to our fathers, to
Abraham and his children forever.

St. Andrew Christmas Novena
*Prayed fifteen times daily, from the Feast of Saint
Andrew (November 30) until Christmas*
Hail, and blessed be the hour and moment
At which the Son of God was born
Of a Virgin most pure
At a stable at midnight in Bethlehem
In the piercing cold.
At this hour vouchsafe, I beseech Thee,
To hear my prayers and grant my desires
(mention request here).
Through Jesus Christ and His most Blessed Mother. Amen.

"The confession of evil works is the first beginning of good works."—*St. Augustine*

Seven Sacraments

Baptism

Confirmation

Eucharist

Reconciliation

Anointing of the Sick

Matrimony (Marriage)

Holy Orders

Ten Commandments

1. I am the Lord your God. You shall not have other gods before Me.
2. You shall not take the name of the Lord your God in vain.
3. Remember to keep Holy the Lord's Day.
4. Honor your father and mother.
5. You shall not kill.
6. You shall not commit adultery.
7. You shall not steal.
8. You shall not bear false witness against your neighbor.
9. You shall not covet your neighbor's wife.
10. You shall not covet your neighbor's goods.

The Two Great Commandments

1. You shall love the Lord, your God, with all your heart, with all your soul, and with all your mind.
2. You shall love your neighbor as yourself.

"The confession of evil works is the first beginning of good works."—St. Augustine

APPENDIX

Suggested Reading and Media

- *My Catholic Family – Sts. Padre Pio & John Vianney DVD's* (The entire DVD set is worthwhile - *EWTN.com*)
- *King of the Golden City* – Mother Mary Loyola (Our preferred version has study material by Janet P. McKenzie)
- *A Reconciliation Reader-Retreat: Read-Aloud Lessons, Stories, and Poems for Young Catholics Preparing for Confession* – Janet P. McKenzie (RACEforHeaven.com)
- *Brother Francis / Forgiven DVD*
- *Guidebook for Confession for Children* – Edited by Beatriz B. Brillantes - Sinag-Tala Publishers, Inc
- *The Most Beautiful Thing in the World* - Susan Brindle / Ann Brindle / Margaret Brindle
- *The Young Life of St. Maria Faustina* - Claire Jordan Mohan
- *Children's Book of Virtues* - Bill Bennett
- *Holy Heroes Audio Cd's* – HolyHeroes.com
- *A Child's Rule of Life* - Robert Hugh Benson – Neumann Press
- *Angel Food for Boys and Girls (Set of four)* – Father Gerald T. Brennan - Neumann Press (read aloud)
- *The Bible,* read aloud daily to your children, starting with the Gospels. (We use both the New American Standard Bible and *Golden Children's Bible,* by Golden Books).

About the Author

Kristen is married to her best friend and business partner, Nathan. They live in Minnesota where they home-school their seven children. Kristen embraces her vocation of wife and mother as her path to holiness. Writing since 2000 and blogging since 2011, with Nate's encouragement, Kristen also leads a mother's group and speaks to women on their path to sainthood through the vocation of wife and mother. This ministry is a passion, but it is secondary to family commitments.

With Nate's technical expertise, Kristen has two websites, kristen. soleyfamily.com and myconfessioncompanion.com; she blogs at kristen-soley.blogspot.com.

Printed in the United States
By Bookmasters